HOW TO SAVE $1,000 THIS WEEK

EASILY SAVE BIG MONEY ON EVERYDAY EXPENSES WITHOUT GIVING UP YOUR DAILY COFFEE

SCOTT ALAN TURNER

ISBN:
Paperback
978-1-64184-081-1

ebook
978-1-64184-082-8

Also by Scott Alan Turner

99 Minute Millionaire
Money A to Z

Meet Scott online and receive free training at
www.ScottAlanTurner.com

Dedication

This book is dedicated to the rebels, the fighters, and #moneyacs who have struggled but will never quit.

For the people who continue on the path towards debt freedom, financial freedom, and building wealth, despite what other people may think.

You are a rock star.
You're in the band.

Contents

Introduction xvii

1. Utilities and Services 1
Getting a Discount 2
Step 1: Find all the companies that bill you 2
Step 2: Do your homework 3
Step 3: Call each company 3
Step 4: Ask for discounts 3
Step 5: If you don't get a deal, get something 5
Step 6: Ask for credit for previous months 6
Other Tips 6
One thing at a time 6
See if early cancellation is worth it 7
Make sure you only get what you need 7
Consider prepaying to save money 8

These steps *will* cut your monthly bills. 9
Mobile Phones 9
Cancel your phone insurance 10
Home Security 11
Utilities. 12
Cable 12
Watch the major networks online for free 13
Streaming services 14
Get an HD antenna. 15
YouTube/Vimeo (free) 16
Redbox. 16
Check out DVDs from the library (free) 16
Not quite ready to commit? 16
Home Phone 17
magicJack. 17
Internet. 18
Buy your own modem 18
Use a mobile hotspot 18
Have a Pro Negotiate Your Bills 19
Saving Steps 20

2. Cars 21
Loans 21
Insurance 22
Shop new providers 22
Raise deductibles 24
Drop collision 25
Cancel Extended Warranty 26
Gas 27
Saving Steps 27

3. **Credit and Banking** 28
Get Your Bank and Credit Fees Waived 28
Use these call scripts 29
Switch to a Credit Union 31
Save with an Online Bank 33
Avoid ATM Fees 34
Save Interest on Credit Cards 35
Cancel Identity-Theft Insurance 36
Increase Your Credit Score 37
What's a good credit score? 38
Evaluate your credit score for free 38
Steps to improve your score 39
Tracking your score 43
Saving Steps 43

4. **Debts** 44
Debt Reduction Methods to Avoid 44
Avoid debt consolidation 45
Avoid debt settlement services 47
Legitimate debt services 48
Refinancing to Reduce Debt 49
Mortgages 50
Student Loans 51
Real Debt Help 55
Saving Steps 55

5. **Shopping** 56
Money-Saving Apps 56
Save Money at Amazon 57
1. Discounted Amazon Gift Cards 57
2. Amazon Outlet 58

3. Trade-in 58
4. Subscribe and Save 59
5. Wait and Save. 59
6. Get Today's Deals. 60
7. Price Guarantee (TVs only) 61
8. Family Savings 61
9. Student Discount 62
10. Amazon Store Card 62
Cancel Unused Memberships. 63
Mystery Shopping 63
Cash for Old Electronics 66
Free Samples. 67
Cancel and Avoid Extended Warranties. 68
Saving Steps 69

6. Housing and Home Maintenance 70
Home Insurance. 70
Save on Rent. 71
Location, location, location 71
Long-term lease. 72
Negotiate lease renewals 72
Move close to public transportation. 73
Shop around for deals 73
Get a roommate. 74
Buy renters insurance 74
Buy Cheap Stuff 75
Outfit Your Kitchen to Save Money 76
Energy Savings. 77
Vampire appliances 77
Stuff your fridge. 77

Pull your fridge out an inch 78
Clean your refrigerator coils. 79
Switch the direction on the ceiling fan 79
Childproof your walls. 80
Tax Benefits and Rebates 80
HVAC Savings 81
Remove shrubs around HVAC 81
HVAC maintenance. 81
Check windows for broken seals 82
Replace your door sweeps. 83
Outside the House 83
Negotiate your lawn care 84
DIY home services. 84
DIY pest control 85
Check sprinklers/change the schedule 85
Install a separate water meter for irrigation 86
Saving Steps 87

7. **Health and Wellness** 88
Life Insurance. 88
Avoid whole life insurance 89
Cancel life insurance for children. 91
Cheaper Prescription Drugs 91
Cancel Unused Gym Memberships 92
Dispute Your Medical Bills. 93
Sign Up for an HSA. 93
Saving Steps 94

8. **Groceries** 95
Before You Shop. 96
Easiest way to save 96

Make a shopping list 97
Use the cash envelope system. 97
Clip coupons 98
Consider memberships. 99
At the Store 99
Compare prices by weight 99
Avoid prepackaged items 100
Reduce meat consumption. 101
Skip bottled water 101
Use a cash-back credit card 102
Don't shop hungry. Or with your kids. 102
Buy store brands. 103
Buy in bulk. 103
At Home 104
Eat what you have 104
Make a few things yourself 104
Rebates on stuff you already bought. 105
Save on Organics 106
Alcohol. 108
Buy at the warehouse clubs 108
Avoid name-brand misconceptions 108
Beware of overhyped brands 109
Other tips. 110
Saving Steps 111

9. Eating Out. 112
Eating Out On a Spending Plan 113
Prioritize your spending. 113
Make a plan 114
Be content 115

Before You Go Out 115
Grab a snack 115
Kids eat free! 116
Get social 116
Pad your stomach with H2O 116
Restaurant clubs 117
Loyalty cards 117
Meal deals 117
Discount gift cards 118
Use coupons 118
Pay with cash 118
When to Eat 119
Lunch is less 119
Eat with the early birds 119
Happy, happy, happy hour 119
Buffets 120
Drinks 120
BYOB 120
Buy the glass 121
Corkage fees 121
Skip the fountain drinks 122
Water 122
Appetizers 123
Ordering 124
Split the check 124
Split an entree 125
Appetizers only 125
Sharing is caring 125
Lunch for a week 125
Chicken is boring (and cheap) 126

Dessert options 126
Check Please 127
Avoid Restaurant Tricks 128
Use overly descriptive language 129
Leave out the dollar sign ($) 130
Highlight items with higher profits 130
Offer dishes in two portion sizes 131
Offer extremely expensive items. 131
Hide value items 132
Use ambiance to increase sales 132
Strategically set the buffet 133
Saving Steps 133

10. Family and Children 134
Shopping for Baby 134
What to buy used. 134
When and where you shop 136
Things to make 137
Things to borrow 138
Things to possibly borrow 139
Things *not* to buy. 140
Tips and tricks 141
Saving Money on Sanity 143
Make Your Own Baby Food 145
Diapers 146
Get free diapers 146
Potty train – now 148
Pets 149
Cancel pet insurance 149
Saving Steps 149

11. Find Extra Money 150
Turn Gift Cards into Cash 150
Bring Home More Money in Your Paycheck 151
Find Missing Money 153
How you can find missing money 154
Is this for every state? 154
How much does it cost? 155
Hidden Discounts 155
Saving Steps 156

12. The Splurge List 157
Things to Splurge On 158
1. Cookware 158
2. Coffee Maker 158
3. Toilet Paper 159
4. Shoes 159
5. Food 159
6. Office Chair 160
What's Not Worth Splurging On 161
1. Pet food 161
2. Mattresses 161
3. Sheets 162
Spending Steps 162

About The Author 165

References 167

Introduction

You can't earn your way to wealth. You have to save something along the way.

I was edging closer to a financial cliff after I bought my first house. Lifestyle creep had set in and I went from living in an expensive apartment and driving a nice car with a big car payment to a big house that came with a big mortgage. I filled it full of furniture and found myself without any savings. In other words, I was like most people—I had some nice stuff, and I was broke.

The paycheck-to-paycheck lifestyle had me trapped in its web.

Something weird happened, though. On my new forty-minute daily commute in Atlanta, I saw a billboard for a talk radio show. When I first started listening to consumer advocate

Clark Howard on the radio, I tried one of his suggestions about locking in my energy rates for a year. I ended up saving a couple hundred bucks as the price of natural gas went up that winter.

I started reading books about saving money and personal finance and a giant world of savings opened up that I never knew existed. By applying some of those ideas, I saved over $1,000 in my first year of owning a home on basic expenses (nothing fancy).

> *How would you feel if you had more money next week? Just imagine the impact it could have.*

People think that if they can just make more money, it will fix their money problems. But what I've experienced in my own life and from coaching listeners of the *Scott Alan Turner Show* is that if people can't manage a little, it will be nearly impossible for them to manage a lot.

When I look at the choice to save money on something like my phone service, I haven't given up anything but I get to keep more of my hard-earned money. How easy is that?

I've been studying money and personal finance for over fifteen years. What you'll find in this book are ideas I've learned from the hundreds of personal finance books I've read and the thousands of hours I've spent listening to radio and podcasts. You'll also get tips from listeners of the *Scott Alan Turner Show*, from my friends and family, and from me, as I relate what I've learned through trial and error. Who doesn't want to keep more of their money instead of handing it over to a company, service, or sales person?

While I occasionally mention these money-saving tips and hacks on the *Scott Alan Turner Show* and have written about them on my blog, this is the first time I've put them all together in one place. Over 100,000 readers and listeners have put these tips to use.

> *We were able to put together $160/month in savings from your tips (That's almost $2000/year!). Mostly, we knew a lot of these things, but the tips were motivating and helped us make the needed phone calls to get it done. We're excited to find more savings! - Walter G.*

What do you know about the benefits of saving? You already know people who spend hours on Sunday clipping coupons to save a couple bucks at the grocery store. If that's your thing and you love the hunt of the deal, I'm happy for you. But that's not what this book is about. This book is about the simple wins you don't practice regularly or have never heard about. It's about saving small amounts of money year after year so that they add up to tens of thousands of dollars over a lifetime. The good news is you're not sacrificing any quality of life. You're just using some common sense money-saving advice your grandmother would have used.

But common sense isn't always common practice, so this book will guide you along the path to big savings.

Think of it this way—it's kinda like if you're walking down the street and you spot a twenty-dollar bill on the sidewalk, and there is nobody around. You pick it up and keep it, right? IT'S FREE MONEY. That's what this book is—a guide for you to get your free money.

Most people are open minded about trying some of these money hacks out. There are quick wins you can do today (easy ones), and there are also tips to help you become more aware of your spending, for bigger wins down the road.

Before we start getting into specific ways to save money, let's make sure you aren't making some common mistakes that can cost you big bucks. I've made these money moron mistakes. Part of my mission is to help others avoid these things.

Mistake #1 We don't know what we don't know.

Wicked clear, right? I don't judge people based on their money mistakes because we've all been there. What's common sense to you now wasn't at one time. Improving with money is like learning how to walk. You get up, fall on your fanny a bunch of times, and then you get good enough to hold on to the coffee table. By age sixteen you can jump hurdles in gym class. Some of what's in this book you may know, some of it you may not (yet). But you'll be a world class sprinter by the last page.

> *I guarantee you don't know the information in the chapter on restaurant tricks. After you read that chapter, you can impress all of your friends the next time you eat out.*

Mistake #2 We aren't consistent with what we do know.

If you own a car, you probably already know you should keep the tires inflated properly by checking them every time you fill up on gas, so the tires last longer, the car runs more smoothly, and you'll save money on gas. But how often do you check your tires? Right, never. Me either.

Air pressure isn't as significant as saving money every month for long-term goals, like a house payment or retirement savings. Most people know they should be saving, yet don't or don't do it consistently for the savings to add up.

Mistake #3 We think small savings don't matter.

Small savings add up to large savings—guaranteed. If you think savings don't matter, go light $1,000 on fire. If you're not willing to do that, then savings *do* matter to you, because that's what these tips will add up to and more.

If you found a $20 bill on the sidewalk every weekend, you'd have a ton of extra money over your life, right? And probably be the luckiest person in the world. But this book isn't about luck. These are real tips to save real money, no luck involved.

Here's what I know—this book will help you become smarter with money. I love this quote from my friend Paula Pant:

> *You can afford anything, you just can't afford everything.*

You already know that you can't buy it all. So, have you thought about what's most important to you? The tips in this book have helped me focus my money on what's important. After many years of stuffing my face with expensive desserts at restaurants (hooray for chocolate cake), I finally came to the realization I'd rather spend half as much and buy a $3.86 pint of Ben & Jerry's ice cream instead. I enjoy a better dessert for half the cost. I call that value-based spending.

You might think that's silly. And you're right, it's a silly example. But for someone who eats out once a week, that's $200 bucks a year in savings, and $2,000 over ten years. Better dessert, less money spent, more money saved—that's the ultimate example of value-based spending in its simplest and easiest form.

When you discover how to do that over and over again, suddenly you've got $2,000 extra a year in your pocket, and $20,000 over ten years. The simple concept of thinking and planning ahead about where to spend the limited dollars we all have increases your savings and helps you win with money.

People that don't figure out what they truly value in life and prioritize their spending accordingly end up being one of the 50 percent of people in their middle age with barely $400 saved for an emergency, and no retirement savings.

There is another word for those people—*broke*. I'm embarrassed to admit it, but even with a good-paying job, I lived paycheck to paycheck.

That's just not what I want for you.

I care about your money, even though I don't know you, because I went through the paycheck-to-paycheck cycle. I experienced lifestyle creep and I accumulated debt. And this message I heard of "save more of what you make" made sense. I took up this mission of helping people like you, and standing with you as you become the champion of your financial journey. I care about what matters to you. I *hate* losing or wasting money (strong words, I know), and I hate it for other people just as much. I remember that sinking feeling you get in your stomach when you realize you've lost money that you didn't have to. It stinks! And I don't want you to feel that way.

I reached financial independence for life in part by using the savings tips in this book, and you can too.

There are two types of people in the world: those who read books like this and do nothing and those who take action with what they have learned and see immediate results.

I bet you're a bit like me—skeptical at first until you see proof. I tell my show listeners all the time to trust but verify. The good news is that I know these tips will help you win with money, as they helped me and my family. Commit to reading them all!

The ideas in this book are simple and easy to do, and best of all, they work! I wish you great success in trying them out.

Have fun and rock on!

- Scott

1

Utilities and Services

Congratulations: you're on your way to taking the steps to save big money. Most people don't take the time to figure out ways to save, but it's quite easy. The goal of this chapter is to get some quick wins and money back in your wallet.

One of the easiest ways you can save money for things like paying off your debts faster is to cut the costs of things you already pay for. You can save hundreds—and sometimes thousands—of dollars a year just by making a few phone calls.

Savings can be just a few minutes away by simply asking for a discount.

> If you own a small business, the savings can get even bigger. Many years ago when I first learned about this technique, I saved nearly $1,000 per month on services I was already using. And all I had to do was ask!

Try these step-by-step instructions (all scripts included!) and you could save yourself thousands of dollars over your lifetime, and probably sooner.

Getting a Discount

Follow these steps to try and get a discount with your current providers. These steps and scripts work!

Step 1: Find all the companies that bill you

Figure out every company you do business with. Dig through your paper pile. Check your bank and credit card statements. Make a big ol' list of everyone.

Everything from:

- electricity
- natural gas/oil
- cell phone
- cable
- Internet
- credit card interest and fees
- bank fees
- insurance (home, auto)
- magazine subscriptions
- gym memberships
- lawn/HVAC/pest control/home services

Step 2: Do your homework

You'll be in a much better position to get a deal and save money if you know there is a deal to be had.

Check the company's website to see what offers and deals they have going on. Many times new customers get better rates than existing customers. No company notifies existing customers like you that prices have dropped. You'll have to find out for yourself.

Don't spend too long, but surf the company's website for a couple of minutes to see what current prices are.

Step 3: Call each company

Start dialing! To save you time, you can try the free service Fast Customer.

Fast Customer lets you select the company you want to speak with.

1. Enter in your phone number
2. A customer service agent will call you – no waiting on hold!

No more wasted time on hold!

Step 4: Ask for discounts

Follow this step-by-step conversation for the best success. I've tried it, and it works!

Please note to be nice to the person on the phone. Chances are they have no authority to give discounts. All they are going to do is answer your question from a prewritten script. It might take ten to thirty minutes to get through to someone that has the power to make a deal. Be polite but firm.

YOU: Hi, I've been a customer for X years, and I'm calling to see what plans are available that will save me money.

THEM: Let me check…

You'll have to wait to see what they come back with.

If they offer you a better deal, woohoo!

If not, you'll have to keep digging.

Keep asking

YOU: What about plans not mentioned on your website?

THEM: No, what we have is listed on the website.

Leverage competitor offers

Most companies have to compete for your dollars. If you have options available to you that you know are better, give your current company a chance to keep your business.

YOU: [COMPETITOR NAME] is offering a better deal on service. I'm thinking about changing services to save some money. What can you do for me?

If you get a discount, awesome. If you're not satisfied and they can't help you, it's time to move on to a supervisor.

THEM: I'm sorry, we're not able to do that.

YOU: I'd like to cancel my service then.

Up until now, you've probably spoken with the entry-level customer support people. They are powerless for the most part. If you tell them you want to cancel, they will probably transfer you to the customer retention department. Getting a deal from them is much more likely.

Once you get to someone that has the power to give you a better deal, ask the same questions. Tell them you found better pricing on their website or a competitor website and want to see what they can do to help you save money.

Leverage your walk-away power

If you are truly willing to leave the company you currently do business with, you have absolute control. If you're just playing them to save money and aren't willing to go, you're less likely to get a deal.

NOTE: They can't cancel your account without your written or verbal permission. Saying "I'd like to cancel my service" doesn't mean you'll get cut off instantly. If you're making a threat to leave, you don't have to follow through.

Step 5: If you don't get a deal, get something

Years ago I called Verizon to get them to lower our TV/Internet/phone bill. However, I wasn't willing to leave them because they had the best Internet service. After thirty minutes on the phone, I managed to get them to give me a one-time credit of thirty dollars.

Get free trials

If you like TV, your cable provider might be willing to give you a free trial of HBO, Showtime, or another movie channel.

Get free add-ons

If you have a DVR or Internet modem, you're probably being charged a hefty fee each month to "rent" the hardware. An Internet modem can run $10/month or $120/year.

Ask what they can do for you to get some savings on hardware rentals.

Step 6: Ask for credit for previous months

If you do get a discount or a new pricing plan, ask if you can have the discount applied retroactively to the previous month or even past several months.

> In a previous business, I noticed my Internet host was charging $25/month for part of my service. I asked to get the service free for the next six months, and for credit for the previous six months as well. They said yes! One simple question saved me $300. Being a loyal, long-term customer can pay off.

Other Tips

Your savings can multiply quickly as you work through all the companies you do business with. Here are a few more money-saving tips:

One thing at a time

If there are several types of discounts that you can potentially get from a company, address them one at a time. Consider a cable company where there might be an opportunity to get a cheaper plan, discounted hardware rental rate (or a few free months), and some trial offers.

Take them One. At. A. Time.

1. First, work the cheaper plan, and get to a yes or no.
2. Then move on to asking about hardware rental, and get to a yes or no.
3. Then move on to discussing trial offers.

If you go in guns blazing and ask for everything at once, you might get one thing. Yes, you'll be happy, but you may miss out on getting so much more.

Follow the scripts.

See if early cancellation is worth it

I once paid an early cancellation fee for Internet service to switch to a lower-cost plan and came out ahead.

You'll have to weigh whether paying the early termination fee and getting into a lower-priced plan makes sense.

For example, say you're paying $60 for cable Internet from AT&T, and you can get $40 Internet from another provider. You'll save $20/month or $240/year. If the early termination fee from AT&T is twice your monthly bill ($60 X 2, or $120), you'll break even after six months if you switch.

Make sure you only get what you need

With cable, Internet, landlines, and cell phones, all the stupid taxes and fees can add up to an *extra $20 to $30/month.*

If you don't need a landline with your Internet service, don't get it.

For example, we have blazing fast Internet for only $40/month with **no extras**.

Consider prepaying to save money

You can save a lot of money by prepaying for services.

Some online services will give you a deep discount if you prepay three, six, or even twelve months in advance. Gyms do this a lot too. My advice is to try the service for three to six months first on a month-to-month plan before committing long term.

I've found that sometimes I think I'll use a service and then stop after a couple of months (*I've learned this lesson the expensive way*). Once I'm sure I'll continue to use a service, I sign up long term.

Insurance policies are another place where prepaying can lead to savings. Car insurance, home insurance, and renters insurance are all types of insurance that you'll likely get a discount for if you pay the policy in full (twelve months) or in part (six months).

Many insurers will hit you with an **extra** dollar or two each month for monthly payments. Plus you might get charged a fee for paying with a credit card or *mailing in your payment.*

With insurance, you don't have to worry about losing money if you cancel your policy before the expiration date. *You'll get a refund for the unused balance.*

These steps *will* cut your monthly bills.

Companies know it's cheaper to keep you as a customer by giving you a discount or helping you save money than it is to pay to get new customers. They want to keep you.

Spend an hour making some phone calls and see what savings you can get. Listeners of the *Scott Alan Turner Show* have saved thousands of dollars doing this on all kinds of services.

Mobile Phones

Your cell phone provider is not loyal to you, and neither should you be to them. Saving money is more important.

It can be worth it to drop your current plan and pay the cancellation penalty if you can save $50/month on the same service from another provider.

Here are the top discount providers:

Cricket

Cricket uses the AT&T cellular network and is much less expensive than AT&T.

> We went from $180+ a month with AT&T to $110 a month with Cricket. They use the same exact network! And Cricket has unlimited everything. AT&T kept raising our rates to force us off their old unlimited plan.

Republic Wireless

Republic Wireless is a unique service that routes calls over Wi-Fi and uses Sprint when you're not near Wi-Fi. You'll have to use their phones though. If you like your iPhone, forget it.

Boost Mobile

Boost Mobile is a sub brand of Sprint. You get unlimited talk, unlimited text, and 2.5 GB of data for $35 a month, and no contract. If you like the Sprint network, check out Boost Mobile.

> You can also compare plans at Whistle Out.

Cancel your phone insurance

If you have a decent phone case, how likely is it you're going to break your phone? The insurance plan on most phones is $10/month. Over the twenty-four months, until you upgrade, that's $240, or the price of your next phone.

Oh, and by the way, your insurance plan usually has a $100 deductible if you break your phone and need a replacement. So on top of the $10/month insurance, you have to pay an additional $100 to get a replacement phone. And the replacement will be:

- Refurbished
- The same version as your current phone

You're paying too much for an outdated replacement phone with this type of insurance.

My wife bought a new iPhone in late 2018, and then dropped it two week later, shattering the screen. Guess who didn't buy the $200 phone insurance? It didn't matter. She found a local repair service that showed up at our house and replaced the screen for $70. That beats the heck out of going back to the Apple store. She can break the screen two more times and we'll still come out better.

Home Security

There is a wide range of home security monitoring services and costs. One of my first money lessons as a homeowner was to ditch the expensive national alarm monitoring services, knocking my monthly bill from $30/month to $15/month, or $180 a year saved. The name-brand services you see advertised on TV are often the most expensive, and they lock people into long-term contracts. Instead of that, consider one of these less expensive options:

Homes with pre-wired systems

Search online for a *local security monitoring company*. They offer the **same** reliable service at **half** the cost. If you're locked into a two-year contract with a national company, make a note on your calendar ninety days before your contract is up.

You will have to follow their termination instructions *to the letter* to avoid being *auto-renewed*. Usually, that involves mailing in something in writing to cancel your contract sixty to ninety days before your renewal date.

Homes with no security systems

SimpliSafe and Ring are two of the largest providers of home security if you want to buy your own hardware, install it, and then pay a low monthly fee. It's a great option if you want to take your hardware with you when you move, or you want to switch from a high-priced provider to a lower monthly cost.

I've used SimpliSafe and they work just as well as any other monitoring service.

The biggest benefits are no contracts and a monthly fee that is half the cost of the big monitoring services.

Utilities

In many areas, there are multiple providers for the electricity, oil, and natural gas that heats and cools your residence. You can save up to 25 percent on your monthly energy bill by switching to a lower-cost provider.

Use Google to search for "local utility providers" to compare rates.

Have your monthly utility bill handy so you can compare the per-kilowatt-hour/natural gas rates.

Cable

The average cable bill is $99.10. That's a whopping $1,200/year, so it's no wonder you might be looking for ways to save money on your cable bill.

Canceling your cable and subscribing to less expensive streaming services can save you big money, and you can still watch your favorite shows.

Getting your favorite shows without the massive cable bill—a.k.a. cord cutting—is extremely popular due to the many options available for watching shows online.

> We got tired of spending $125/month on cable TV ($1,500 per year) and canceled our cable service. We currently subscribe to two services (Amazon Prime and Netflix), which cost us $18 per month. Even when you add in what we pay for the Internet ($40 per month), that's still a savings of $750 per year!

You might have access to 500 channels, but how many do you watch? Does it really matter to you whether you can watch a show as soon as it comes out? Most people enjoy the savings enough that they are willing to wait to watch certain shows.

Watch the major networks online for free

Most networks include streaming of current episodes directly from their websites. You will have to sit through the commercials just like with cable.

- NBC
- CBS
- Fox
- ABC

Newer smart TVs come with apps for the major networks so you can watch them on TV as you normally would. There is also an option to cast your videos from a laptop, tablet, or smartphone and watch it on a TV.

Streaming services

Here are the top providers of streaming content. Using one, two, or even three streaming services is often cheaper than cable. Prices vary and sometimes include special offers and free trials so check each provider's website.

If you have a new smart TV, all of these services can be installed just like an app on your phone. The apps stream content directly from the Internet without any special hardware. If you have an older TV, you may need to by an Amazon Fire TV Stick, Roku, or Chromecast device first ($24.00–$35.00).

Hulu – Hulu offers hundreds of thousands of hours of the best of current season programming, premium original content, films, and full seasons of hit series to subscribers with limited commercials for $7.99 per month or commercial-free for $11.99 per month.

Amazon Prime – Lots of original content, Thursday night football, old HBO hit series, and tons more. Plus, you get the other benefits of Amazon Prime, such as two-day shipping and lots of other bonus features.

Netflix – Netflix doesn't have any commercials. Most devices you have in your house (Blu-ray players, gaming consoles, Amazon Fire TV, Chromecast) probably have the Netflix app preloaded.

Sling TV – Sling TV is the next best thing to cable TV without the price. Stream your favorite live shows, sports, news, and hit movies instantly on ESPN, AMC, CNN, HGTV, Comedy Central, Cartoon Network, History, Disney, and more. If sports are important to you or your significant other, Sling Blue includes local sports, as well, for an added cost.

HBO NOW – HBO NOW lets you stream all of HBO's programming instantly with unlimited access to their popular programs and movies. Sling TV also comes with an option to add HBO programming for an additional charge per month.

Get an HD antenna

Your one worry about canceling cable may be not being able to watch your favorite sports teams live. Enter the HD antenna, which will pick up local stations. You'll even be able to watch the local news, soap operas in the afternoon, and Wheel of Fortune.

HD antennas have come a long way since they were introduced. Some are powered to provide an additional boost to incoming signals.

We have one mounted on our wall, and it picks up the local stations (NBC, CBS, ABC, Fox) just fine. We also get about thirty other random stations that have older programming, movies, shopping channels—the list goes on.

Don't expect to get any of the common network shows you'll find on cable, though. You won't find Food Network or HGTV on the antenna.

What about recording?

HD antennas can be plugged into a TiVo box. You can also get full DVR scheduling and recording on all available over-the-air channels from AntennaWeb.org.

YouTube/Vimeo (free)

Documentaries? Concerts? Educational programs? Besides dancing bears and crazy car chases, YouTube has a lot of longer content to entertain and educate (*like The Scott Alan Turner Show*).

Redbox

Redbox is a DVD rental service that uses outdoor vending machines. It's available at Walmart, CVS, Walgreens, and many other places. For two dollars you can rent recent movies as a DVD. The machines resemble soda machines and are bright red, which makes them hard to miss.

Check out DVDs from the library (free)

The library is a great place to get not only books but audio books and DVDs. Many libraries have a lending program that will transfer items from a different branch if you can't find what you're looking for at your branch (as long as they are in the same network/community).

When my wife and I first got married, I would drive my scooter to the library and check out DVDs. We didn't have cable, as Katie was going to school at night, and we didn't watch much TV back then.

Not quite ready to commit?

If you still aren't ready to give up cable, call your current provider and ask for a lower rate. Tell them you're thinking of canceling because you're looking to save money. Once you get transferred to the customer retention department, you'll be able to get a deal.

When you have decided now is the time, add up the cost of the streaming services you want to use and your monthly Internet charges to *make sure you aren't paying more than your current cable bill.*

Home Phone

If you have a landline or one of those triple-play combos for cable/internet/phone, decide if you need a landline. Chances are you can get by with just a cell phone. If you do need a home phone line, check out switching to one of the following:

magicJack

- Unlimited local and long-distance calling to the US, Canada, Puerto Rico, and the US Virgin Islands
- No contract, no monthly bills
- Works with your Internet connection
- Get the magicJack device and a year of service for only $39.00.

MagicJack.com

Vonage

- $9.99/month for a twelve-month contract.
- Unlimited calling to over sixty countries. Great for international use.

Vonage.com

Internet

Here are a couple tips to save on your Internet each month.

Buy your own modem

If you're paying for Internet, you're probably paying a separate monthly fee for the privilege of renting a modem from your provider. If you buy your own modem, you can recoup the cost in as little as a year—and then start saving anywhere from $6 to $10 each month.

If you have a cable modem, check out Wirecutter's write-up of the best cable modem based on your Internet provider.

Another option is to look at your current brand and model number and buy an identical make/model off of eBay. Once you get your new one set up, call your Internet provider and tell them you don't want to rent your modem anymore. They will give you instructions to ship it back or drop it off at a local authorized dealer.

> I have my own modem for my Internet service, and it saves me $110/year in rental fees.

It might take six months to one year for the modem to pay for itself but after that, you'll be able to pocket the savings.

Use a mobile hotspot

You already know how to use your smart phone to access the Internet. A mobile hotspot does the same thing, except you attach it to your laptop. It looks like a little USB stick.

Wherever you have Internet on your phone, you could have Internet for your laptop.

Karma is a mobile hotspot you could consider as a replacement for your cable/DSL/satellite Internet connection. The best part is, if you travel, you can take your Karma hotspot with you. No more $15/night Internet charges at hotels!

The Karma device is $199.

- Get worry-free Internet access for as little as $3/month
- Compare that to the AT&T mobility hotspot, which costs $25/month for the same service

Because it has a money-back guarantee, it's worth trying out to see what you think of the performance.

Have a Pro Negotiate Your Bills

Finally, if you love your current cable and cell phone services and can't get them to budge, let the professional negotiators have at it.

BillFixers.com is a service that will try to negotiate lower rates on your behalf. You send them a copy of your bill, and they do the rest. *Don't worry*—they won't change your current plan or service.

> I tried BillFixers to get a lower rate on my AT&T cell phone bill. Since I was already on a good plan, they were not able to lower my bill. But it was worth a try.

Saving Steps

- List all of the utilities and services you use and call each company
- If you can't get a discount, get something
- Keep trying this for the rest of your life

Turn the page and let me show you how to save money on cars.

2

Cars

Vehicles are one of your biggest expenses, and it frustrates me hearing from people who are saddled with big debts from their autos. There are many ways to save on your existing car. Plus, I have tips on the types of insurance you don't need, and much more.

Loans

Eighty percent of car purchases are financed at the dealership. However, credit unions offer interest rates that can be as much as *2.5 percent less* than other lenders. If you have a car loan, it's worth a phone call to a local credit union to see if they will refinance your loan.

Consider that the average amount borrowed for a car is $31,000, and the average car payment is $523/month.[1] An interest rate that is 2.5 percent lower would save the average owner $2,103 over the sixty-month term!

Don't extend the term! If you have thirty-six months left on your loan, you want a new thirty-six-month loan with a lower rate. If you extend your current term (to forty-eight months, sixty months, or more), you'll likely end up paying even more in interest.

Check with online lenders too at bankrate.com

Insurance

Some people go **years and years** and **never** check their coverage or shop around for lower rates.

You could potentially save **$1,000 or more per year** on your auto insurance by following these tips, so don't miss out. I wish I'd had this information years ago and, chances are, so will you!

Shop new providers

When was the last time you shopped around for better insurance rates?

Car insurance is very competitive. You've seen the TV ads, right?

- Are you in good hands?
- Fifteen minutes could save you fifteen percent or more!

Your credit score, your education, what you do for work—they all factor into your insurance rates. One insurance carrier *may charge more than twice what another does for the exact same coverage for the same person.*

You could **save $100 or more per month** just by spending fifteen minutes shopping around.

You should check with ALL of the following to find the best deal. Several big name insurance providers (State Farm, Geico) DO NOT participate in the online quote comparison websites, so you will need to check their websites directly.

- Insure.com
- Esurance
- State Farm
- Geico
- Call a local insurance broker

Avoid poorly rated insurance companies

When you shop around, price is not the only thing you should consider. Using a highly rated insurance company is also important.

If you are with a highly ranked insurer and you find a quote that is only slightly less expensive from a lower-rated company, stick with the better company even though it costs more.

According to Consumer Reports, the top insurers are

1. Amica Insurance
2. USAA Property and Casualty
3. New Jersey Manufacturers Insurance Company
4. Auto-Owners Insurance

The lowest-rated auto insurers in the country are

1. Allstate Insurance
2. Farmers Insurance
3. Travelers
4. MetLife Auto & Home

Ask your existing insurer for a discount

If you're happy with your current insurance company but find a lower offer from another insurer, *ask* your current insurer to match the deal you found.

If they're smart, they will match the rates to keep you as a customer.

If they aren't, it's time for you to change and save some money.

Use one insurance company

By keeping your home, auto, and renters insurance with one company, you'll often get a **10–20 percent discount**.

> When I re-shopped my insurance in December 2015, I saved thirty percent on my new policies.

Raise deductibles

Your deductible is the amount of money you pay out of pocket if you get in an accident. Most people go with the lowest deductible available, which increases your annual premiums.

How much should you have for a deductible?

First, you need to make sure you have enough money in your emergency fund to cover the cost of your deductible in case of an accident. If you haven't started your emergency fund, it doesn't make sense to increase your deductible to an amount you don't have readily available.

For the best savings on auto insurance, a **deductible of $1,000** will allow you to have **lower premiums**.

Additionally, if you get in a minor fender-bender, you are better off paying out of pocket. If you make a claim for a small amount to your insurer, your rates will probably *increase*. Since you will probably have to pay the total cost of a small accident anyway (because of the higher deductible), there is no point in submitting to the insurance company.

Never file an insurance claim for inexpensive problems like a cracked windshield or a scratched bumper. The insurance company will raise your premiums next year by as much as 25 percent or, even worse, cancel your policy.

Drop collision

When is the last time you checked your auto policy for what types of coverage you have? If you are paying for collision coverage, consider if it is worth it.

Collision insurance covers a car if it is in an accident with another car or a fixed object, such as a tree or a barricade. If you are driving an older car or a junker and you are in an accident, the cost of repairs would probably exceed the value of the car. The insurance adjuster would declare the car a total loss. After your deductible, you wouldn't collect an amount equal to your payments.

The general rule is that if your car is worth less than ten times the cost of the combined annual collision and comprehensive insurance, you're better off dropping collision insurance.[2]

Cancel Extended Warranty

Consumer Reports found some surprising stats when they researched extended auto warranties:

- 55 percent of people who bought an extended warranty never used it.
- Of the 45 percent who did use it, on average, they spent more on the warranty than it paid for in repairs.[3]
- On average, people who bought an extended warranty had a net loss of more than $375 when comparing the warranty cost with the repair cost.[4]

The amount of money you will spend on extended auto warranties over your lifetime will far exceed the benefit. You are better off putting the money you would have spent on the warranty in a savings account instead and paying for any repairs yourself.

If you currently have an extended warranty on your car, see if you can get reimbursed for the unused balance and, if so, cancel it. If you can't, make a note to not renew it again.

It sounds like a good deal, but when you figure *30–40 years* of car ownership, the math is not in your favor.

> Make sure to have enough cash in an emergency fund to cover repairs that may come up.

Gas

Gas Buddy is a free app providing real-time gas prices so that consumers can locate the lowest fuel prices available.

Where I live, I've seen gas prices at stations less than a mile from each other vary by as much as $0.25 a gallon.

With the average person driving 12,000 miles per year, and the average car getting 24 mpg, that's a quick and easy $125 in savings.

Saving Steps

- See if you can refinance any existing loans to a lower rate
- Shop around for new car insurance
- Never buy an extended warranty again

Now let's get back those pesky fees the banks and credit card companies keep charging us.

3

Credit and Banking

It seems every week another big bank is getting hit with a multi-million dollar fine for taking advantage of customers. Banks are supposed to provide a checking, savings, or credit accounts, and be in the business of lending money. Instead they make billions of dollars by charging customers fees, fees, and more fees. It's like moving into an apartment and then being charged extra for the carpet and the air you breath each month. There is a better way.

Get Your Bank and Credit Fees Waived

Do you hate getting hit with late fees, overdraft fees, and other fees? Sometimes it feels like we're getting fee'd to death.

For example, you can get hit with an overdraft fee if you overspend in your checking account. Your bank conveniently transfers money from your savings account or credit card to cover the cost.

Banks love overdraft fees! According to a report by Pew Charitable Trusts, the largest US banks charged $11.6 billion in overdraft fees and insufficient fund fees in 2015. According to the report, most of the people paying the billions of dollars in overdraft fees are young and have lower incomes.

But the good news is you can often get your money back by calling your bank or credit card issuer and just *asking* for a refund.

Check your credit cards and bank statements for fees that could be waived:

- late fees
- overdraft fees
- monthly maintenance fees
- annual dues

Use these call scripts

If you've made an honest mistake, use these scripts to get those annoying bank and credit card fees refunded.

YOU: I was charged a late fee/annual fee/overdraft on my account that I would like removed because I'm an awesome customer.

THEM: All of our customers are awesome. I'll be glad to see what I can do.

Seriously, that's what I did.

Or you might get the following:

THEM: Sorry there is nothing we can do.

Wait! Don't give up. What power do you have?

- Are you a longtime customer?
- Are you a profitable customer?
- Are you a business customer?

If you answered yes to any of those questions, you've got a little power, so try again. Leverage what you've got. If you've got nothing, try anyway.

Banks and credit card companies can pay five to twenty-five times more to replace you as a customer. They want to keep you, so waiving a fee can be a small price to pay.

YOU: Well, I've been a customer for two years. What can you do for me?

And see what they come back with. If your credit card or bank account has overdraft fees, you can try the same scripts out. You can try the same thing with bank charges.

> I forgot to pay my credit card bill on time (happens to the best of us, ha-ha). I had just charged all of my yearly insurance payments (two homes, two autos, umbrella policy, boat), Katie's trip to Japan, plus our normal monthly charges. I was hit with a $287 interest charge, and a $25 late fee. The script I listed above is exactly what I said.
>
> I called Capital One, was transferred around (because you have to work your way up the food chain to someone with authority to waive fees) and was on the phone for thirty minutes.

Because I am a valued customer, the charges were dropped.

What NOT to say

The scripts above are a good guideline. Here are a few more tips for success.

- **Be polite, but firm.** The customer service rep is usually a small cog in a big machine. They have limits to what they can offer. Ask to speak to a supervisor if the rep can't help you.
- **Shut up.** State your request and be quiet. You don't need to explain every detail about why the company should waive the fee in ten minutes. State your request and wait.
- **Don't give them a chance to say no.** *"What can you do for me"* is an open-ended question that allows the customer rep some options. *"Can you waive this fee"* has only two outcomes—**yes** or **no**. Since you're trying to *avoid no*, it's better to avoid yes/no questions.

Your turn: Check your last three months of bank and credit card statements for any overdraft fees, late fees, or interest charges. Sometimes the charges can slip by. With a quick phone call, you can have that money back in your pocket where it belongs.

Switch to a Credit Union

Credit unions are customer-owned banks, and they tend to offer lower fees on services and lower interest rates than standard banks. Credit unions are a bit like clubs in that not just anyone can join. Each credit union serves what's called their "field of membership"—that's the commonality between the members. For example, some large organizations have a credit union for their employees (e.g., American Airlines does). For others, you will have to see what their requirements are and determine if you qualify.

Most of the monster mega-banks give paltry interest rates (i.e., *zero percent*) on checking and savings accounts. And they generally rate poorly on customer service. By joining a credit union you will get:

- Better service
- Better loan rates for autos and homes
- Lower/no fees
- Interest on your checking/savings accounts

You can find a credit union in your area with this location tool.

Also, check out PenFed. It's easy to sign up online. If you meet their eligibility requirements (e.g., you're a military member, you work for the US government, or you belong to a qualifying association), it's worth the small one-time fee for all the savings you'll get.

This listener of my show explains the benefits of a credit union best:

> *I ended up choosing a credit union that met all of my criteria (local branches, good banking products, great rates). My experience thus far has been absolutely amazing!!*
>
> - *They know my name and greet me as soon as I walk into the branch.*

- *They treat me like a lifelong friend: Ask about the kids, mention local community events, lunch recommendations.*
- *In my first month, my monthly profit sharing/dividend credit was larger than what my old big bank paid me for the past 18 months.*
- *I'm not nickel and dimed to death. Cashier's checks, Money wires, bill pay, etc. are done at no charge.*
- *I get "just checking in" calls regularly from the branch manager asking how they can improve their service.*

Some lowlights:

- *I feel like an idiot for not doing this a decade ago.*

If you are still banking with the big banks, you are being taken advantage of. Stop being part of the problem and supporting the bad guys. Move your money to a local bank or credit union. Support your communities, support small business, support yourself with increased value.

Omid, California, Scott Alan Turner Show listener

Save with an Online Bank

Going online with your savings has several benefits, like lower fees, increased interest, and lower-cost services. If a credit union or local bank doesn't appeal to you, consider an online bank.

I've been with CapitalOne360 (formerly ING) for nearly a decade. Why switch?

- **No minimum balances.** Brick-and-mortar banks like Chase can charge $5/month if you hold less than $300 in your account. That's $60/year you're losing.
- **More interest.** Right now, brick-and-mortar banks give you slightly more than 0 percent for your balance in checking and savings. An online bank is currently paying out 1 percent. If you have $20,000 in your emergency fund, you could be earning up to $200/year in interest.
- **Multiple savings accounts for free.** In my CapitalOne360 account, I can set up multiple savings accounts very quickly. I keep separate accounts for my emergency fund and several savings goals. It makes it easy to keep track of your money. Some banks will charge a fee every month for every account.

If you want to explore all the different savings accounts offered by banks, take a look at bankrate.com.

Avoid ATM Fees

Your bank likely gives you access to ATMs located all throughout its network. What happens when you visit an ATM outside of your network? Usually you'll get hit with a fee of $4.50 or more per withdrawal.[5] Using an out-of-network ATM just once a month would cost you over $50 a year in fees.

To avoid ATM fees, one of my favorite checking accounts is the Discover Cashback Rewards Checking Account from Discover Bank. This account gives you access to over 68,000 ATMs for free. It also gives you ten cents back on every debit card purchase.

While local banks and credit unions sometimes provide free checking accounts, many do not provide you with the ability to get cash out of other banks' ATMs without a charge. Discover's network of ATMs allows you to take money out of various ATMs at locations near you at no additional charge.

Save Interest on Credit Cards

If you're in debt, lowering or eliminating your interest rates is a great way to accelerate your debt-payoff plan. The most obvious way to reduce the interest you are paying on credit cards is to do a balance transfer from a card with a high interest rate to a card with a low interest rate. All this means is that you move the balance you have on one card to another card.

Balance transfer credit cards will often charge you a fee. The Chase Slate card appears to have no balance transfer fees for the first sixty days. It also provides you with twelve months of 0 percent APR on your balance transfer.

While balance transfer cards will often provide you with an introductory rate of 0 percent, the rate will rise **significantly** once the initial period is over. In fact, credit card issuers are counting on people not paying off the balance in full, and then socking them with the new higher interest rates.

A good strategy would be to pay off the high-interest credit card with a balance transfer from the 0 percent card, then commit to pay off the entire balance within the 0 percent introductory period. If you still have a balance outside of the introductory period, you could face interest charges in the 15 percent to 25 percent range. *Not good.*

Another strategy is to use the scripts above to ask for a lower interest rate. Make a list of all your debts and call up each lender to ask if they will lower the interest rate.

> One listener to the *Scott Alan Turner Show* had $60,000 in credit card debt. He was able to get Bank of America to lower his credit card interest rates to just over 3 percent, which allowed him to pay off his debts.

Cancel Identity-Theft Insurance

Identity theft is the fastest growing white-collar crime. In 2017 over 16 million people had their IDs stolen.[6] Identity thieves typically take out credit or loans in another person's name and then goes on a shopping spree. Or they might open an account in someone else's name, such as an Amazon or PayPal account.

There are companies selling identity-theft insurance products with "$1 million in protection" that prey on the fear of consumers and assure them they will be "protected" if a thief steals their identity.

These products are garbage. As a consumer advocate, I've never recommended these products to my listeners.

Here's what consumer advocate Clark Howard had to say about LifeLock,[7] a popular provider of identity-theft insurance:

> While they're a legitimate business, they're also one of the most overhyped services out there. They sell into the fear about you having your identity stolen.
>
> Want more meaningful protection from identity theft than LifeLock has to offer? Do a credit freeze.

If you live in the United States, you can get a credit freeze for free. A credit freeze offers better protection, and it's free. A credit freeze locks down your credit so nobody can open an account in your name. Credit freezes can be done at all major credit bureaus by visiting their websites (Experian, TransUnion, Equifax).

An identity-theft monitoring service is like an alert you get on your phone letting you know you've been robbed. A credit freeze is like a steel cage around your home to keep the bad guys out so you can't get robbed in the first place.

I've had a credit freeze on my personal information for over fifteen years. In fact, I tested it out once to determine if I could open a credit card from both Bank of America and Capital One with my credit freeze in place. Couldn't do it. I know more about myself than any thief ever could, but I still couldn't steal my own information. Case closed.

Increase Your Credit Score

A good credit score gives you access to credit with the best interest rates, allowing you to refinance or borrow and **save on interest**.

> *Lower interest rates can save you tens of thousands of dollars over your lifetime.*

This is especially true when it comes to mortgages, which can take decades to pay off.

What's a good credit score?

The most common credit score, the FICO score, ranges from 300 to 850. If you have a score below 650, you may find it difficult to open new lines of credit or you may pay more for things like car loans, mortgages, and insurance.

Evaluate your credit score for free

Credit Sesame allows you to sign up and get a free credit score report card and an unofficial credit score. You simply go to the site and enter your email address and some personal information to help them pull your credit information. They then put together your credit score report card.

On the card, they give you a grade, A through F, on each of the factors used to calculate your credit score. This allows you to easily see what you're doing well and what areas need improvement. They will even provide tips on *how you can improve your credit score.*

> *My financial path may sound familiar: some credit card debt that went into collections, followed by $30,000 of student loans for a degree I hoped would lead to a great paying career.*
>
> *I vowed to turn my situation around and get out of debt. A friend told me about* Credit Sesame. *I signed up for a free membership and found my credit score was in the low 400s.*
>
> *After downloading the* Credit Sesame app *and following the tips, I improved my score by **217 points.***
>
> *-Brandi*

Your credit score doesn't matter unless it's bad. When it's bad, you need to take action and improve your score.

Steps to improve your score

Your credit score factors in several things. By focusing on these areas, you can raise your score.

1. **Credit Utilization** - how much of your credit lines are you using?
2. **Payment History** - do you pay your bills on time?
3. **Credit Inquiries** - how many hard checks have you had on your credit recently?
4. **Credit Age** - what is the average age of your accounts?
5. **Account Mix** - do you have different kinds of credit?

Your credit utilization and payment history have the biggest impact on your credit score.

Here's how you can improve on each factor used to calculate your credit score.

1. Credit Utilization

Your credit utilization primarily relates to your high revolving debt, such as credit card debt. For example, if you have a credit card with a limit of $10,000 and you have a balance of $2,500 then you have a 25 percent credit utilization.

People with good credit scores keep their credit utilization below 30 percent. People with excellent credit scores keep their utilization below 10 percent.

So how do you lower your credit utilization? There are two ways.

First, *pay down your debt.* If you are carrying a balance on your credit card, try to pay it down. If you pay off your balance each month, that's great. But you could still have a high debt utilization if you max your card out each month.

The second way to lower your debt utilization is to get a higher credit limit. Take our example from earlier. If you get a higher credit limit, say $20,000, that same $2,500 balance is now representing only a 12.5 percent credit utilization.

As you pay down debt, you may see your credit providers automatically extending your line of credit. The higher credit lines can help you to raise your score faster.

Only increase your credit limit if you are sure that you have the willpower not to use the increased limit. Someone who has a history of maxing out their credit cards might not want to tempt themselves with more credit (and obviously it would defeat the purpose if they maxed out their new limit).

> If you are going to ask for a higher credit limit, make sure you are likely to get the higher limit. Typically, if you ask for an increased credit limit, your credit card company or bank will likely run a credit check, which is known as a hard check. A hard check on your credit can reduce your credit score by a few points over a short period. However, lowering your credit utilization will more than make up for the few points from a hard credit check.

Action Point: Pay off debt or raise your credit limit

2. Payment History

The biggest factor in improving your credit score is making payments on time. Paying your credit card bill, auto loan, mortgage, and student loans on time are key. To make sure the minimums are always paid on time, consider using one of these methods:

- Use auto pay
- Set up reminders
- Pay the bills on the same day each month

Make sure you make all your payments on time from now on. With time, your credit score will improve. Even if you just pay the minimums, never miss a date and your credit score will thank you!

Action Point: Make on-time payments

3. Credit Inquiries

Credit inquiries refer to hard checks on your credit. These typically occur when you apply for more credit either through a new loan (like a car loan) or a credit line increase.

However, they can also result from requesting an insurance quote or applying for a new apartment. Try to keep from having too many hard checks done within a year.

If you absolutely must get a car, do all of your shopping around within a week. Credit bureaus know that you are likely looking for the best rate and not actually looking to get six car loans. The bureaus will count all these checks as one check rather than six.

Action Point: If you must have a hard check on your credit score, keep them to a small window of no more than one or two weeks.

4. Credit Age

You can keep your credit score good by not opening new accounts. A new account will bring down the average age of your accounts. Opening lots of new accounts is viewed negatively by the credit reporting bureaus.

For example, if you have one account that is ten years old and one that is five years old, and you open a new account, the average age of the accounts would be five years. However, if you open two new accounts, the average age would drop to *3.75 years*.

Action Point: If you must open a new account, keep it to one account, but try to avoid opening any while you work to raise your score.

5. Account Mix

Your account mix refers to the types of accounts you have. For once, your student loans could be helping your credit score. If you have a credit card and a student loan, then you have two types of credit.

Action Point: By keeping your accounts in good standing and making on-time payments you are demonstrating that you can be responsible with different kinds of credit.

Fixing errors

Errors can have a huge impact on your credit score, and they can easily be corrected by contacting the credit reporting agency. An example is an account on your file that you don't own.

If you have an error on your credit report, you can dispute it.

I contacted the credit bureaus to fix an error and within 30 days my score increased by 100 points.

- Sean, listener of the Scott Alan Turner Show

Tracking your score

Once you start taking action to improve your credit score, make it a habit to track your progress. Credit Sesame will show you how you progress.

The more you progress, the more motivated you will be to keep improving your score! Also if you want to get another mortgage at some point in the future, you'll have less work to do to improve your score if you monitor it.

Saving Steps

- Make the calls to get lower rates and your money back
- Switch to a bank where you're a name and not a number
- Stop wasting money on identity-theft products
- Improve your credit score

Next you'll learn the debt-payoff strategies that don't work and the ones that can save you huge amounts of money on wasted interest payments.

4

Debts

It's infuriating to me that scammers and companies take advantage of people who are barely scraping by. People think companies are out to help them, but in reality they are only out to help themselves—to other people's money! It's frustrating. We feel trapped, with no way out and nobody to help us. There is.

Most people know getting out of debt is the first step on the road to financial freedom, security, and wealth building. People with existing debt have some options available to speed up their plan to become debt-free. This section deals with big expenses, starting with some warnings to keep people out of more debt trouble.

Debt Reduction Methods to Avoid

Debt consolidation and debt settlement services are two ways to get out of debt that you may have heard of. There are frequent commercials touting these methods that make them sound like the holy grail for people in debt. Don't believe the hype.

I do NOT recommend either debt consolidation or debt settlement as a way to save you money. Both are likely to cost you MORE money.

As the *defender of your dollars*, it's my sworn duty to make sure you understand the problem with these services so you don't get ripped off.

Avoid debt consolidation

Debt consolidation takes all of your debts and rolls them up into one smaller, "more manageable" monthly payment. Debt consolidation seems like an answer to some people's prayers. Until they look under the hood. There are gremlins that can cause it to worsen their debt nightmare.

Let's say you have six credit cards with balances. A debt consolidator would take all six balances and create a monthly payment that is lower than all of the minimum monthly payments combined.

Lower payments sound great, don't they?

On the surface it sounds great because they promise to:

- Stop the bill collectors from calling
- Give someone a chance to get back on their feet
- Reduce stress
- Leave them with more money to spend

Who wouldn't want these things if they were in debt?

And you *will* get all these things if you consolidate your debts. But watch out for the gotchas. Consider a couple where one of them lost their job. They have the following two loans, which they are now struggling to keep up with:

- $20,000 on a 4-year loan at 10 percent
- $15,000 on a 3-year loan at 12 percent

The monthly payment on the 4-year loan is *$507.*
The monthly payment on the 3-year loan is *$498.*

The friendly debt consolidator comes along and says:

Hey folks, I've got great news. You're currently paying $1005 a month, but I've talked with the lenders and I can get you a reduced interest rate and get your monthly payment down to $630 at only 9 percent interest!

Sweet! They're thinking "We'll have an extra $400 in our pockets each month." And this is true.

But...

They get the lower monthly payment by spreading out the payments over a longer time. If the loans are paid back over six years, instead of the original loan terms (three years and four years), that results in them paying:

$10,424 in interest for the new longer loan versus $7,238 for the original loans.

They will pay an **extra $3,000 in interest** for the privilege of spreading out the payments.

Does that sound like a deal?

It's going to cost them an extra $3,000.

Avoid debt settlement services

If you're a night owl, you might see these cheesy commercials with the screaming sales pitchman about how debt settlement services can get you out of debt for pennies on the dollar and keep you out of bankruptcy.

Debt settlement is when a creditor agrees to take less than you owe. That sounds great, doesn't it?

It's a scam.

I've heard of a lot of scams, but I tell you, this one is despicable. Scratch that; it's downright unforgivable.

> "It is an outrage that unscrupulous debt settlement companies are allowed to peddle their false promises and take the last dollars from working families that have fallen on hard times." - Sally Greenberg, executive director of the National Consumers League.[8]

If you're asking, *"Is debt settlement right for me*?" let me make this crystal clear: **NO!**

Here's how this works. Your credit card companies aren't going to agree to take less than you owe unless it seems you won't pay at all. So, companies that promise debt settlement typically tell you to stop paying your credit card bills and wait for Visa or MasterCard to cry uncle and agree to work with you. Will this work? Maybe. But while you're doing this, you're running up late fees and interest on your cards. You're incurring **more debt** in the process. And the debt settlement companies are going to charge you big up-front fees to negotiate the new terms with the credit card companies on your behalf, as well as monthly fees after that.

It's all smoke and mirrors, folks. The high fees from the settlement company and the increased debt from the late fees and credit card interest negate any savings you may get from the settlement.

Please don't fall for these scammers. They are not out to help you. It's easy to fall prey to the hope they are promising, but the reality is much different than the promises.

Legitimate debt services

I understand some people have reached the end of their rope and are looking for a lifeline. They may be unable to make it work in their situation. Not everyone can follow the one-size-fits-all cookie-cutter solutions.

For those who have decided that the only way to get out of debt is debt consolidation, it would be a disservice if I didn't tell you about *legitimate* companies that do this.

Again, **I don't recommend debt consolidation**. It doesn't fix the problem (which is often poor spending habits), and in the end it increases the debts. But if you feel you must go ahead with debt consolidation, one legitimate service is the National Foundation for Credit Counseling (NFCC). You can reach them at their website or you can call 1–800–388–2227. NFCC offers free or low-cost debt counseling and debt management plans. About one in three of NFCC clients just needs some budgeting help to get their lives back on track. *I have no affiliation with NFCC.*

> "Since I started listening to your show, I went from having about $600 dollars to my name to $36,000 today. I was paying a credit card repair company. I thought they were helping but they never did. I'm glad you told me about NFCC.org" – G, NYC

Refinancing to Reduce Debt

While debt consolidation doesn't work to reduce debt, refinancing does. You could be saving a lot of money each month and over the life of your loans by refinancing. Refinancing your student loans, car loan, or mortgage will not only help you save money, but it will also help you get out of debt and achieve financial freedom faster.

The key is discipline. The mistake too many people make is to refinance to a lower monthly payment, but then stretch out the payments over a longer period of time. This results in them paying more in interest, which increases debt instead of decreasing debt.

Here's an example:

With a starting loan balance of $35,000 and term of ten years @ 5.7%, if all you did was refinance to a lower interest rate of 4.99% **you would save $1,471** if the new loan had the same ten-year term.

But stretch your new loan out to twelve years, and you will pay an **extra $591**!

The goal of refinancing loans is to *save money*, and that's it. You save money by getting a lower interest rate and keeping the term the same or shorter than your original loan.

What if the only option is for a longer term? Often you'll find when you try to refinance that you can only get a lower interest rate if you lengthen the term. The lender makes money by stretching out your payments over a longer term.

1. You can still save money! Two things must be true:
2. You must have discipline

There must be no prepayment penalty on your refinanced loan

Pretend you refinance the $35,000 loan mentioned above from 5.7 percent to 4.99 percent and the new term is twenty years long.

Even though your interest rate has gone down, the extra ten years of payments will cost you an **additional $9,392**.

But if you continue to pay your new loan by sending in the same monthly payment as you were before refinancing, you will both save money **and** have the loan paid off in **fewer than ten years**.

Mortgages

Mortgages are most people's biggest expense. If you already have a mortgage, refinancing to a lower interest rate could save tens of thousands, even hundreds of thousands of dollars, in interest payments.

Generally, the math is in your favor to refinance if:

- you can get refinanced for a new rate that is 1 percent less than your current rate

- AND you can roll the closing costs into your new mortgage
- AND you stay in your home long enough to break even (two to five more years)

Call your local bank's loan officer and ask them to walk you through the math to see if it makes financial sense.

Just as I mentioned before, refinancing works to save you money when you refinance to a lower payment *but you keep paying what you were before*. Here's an example:

If you have twenty-six years left on your mortgage, and you refinance to a new thirty-year loan with a lower interest rate, you could end up paying more in interest if you pay for the next thirty years. However, if you keep sending in the old (higher) monthly mortgage payment, as if your new loan still had twenty-six years left on it, you end up paying less in interest.

Check bankrate.com for current interest rates.

> I refinanced my first house twice in a five-year period and saved thousands in interest charges and PMI (private mortgage insurance).

Student Loans

Students graduating with student loans owe an average of $35,051.

When I paid my first student loan bill, I was shocked a measly one dollar went towards principal, and the rest went towards interest.

Refinancing your student loans will help you pay down the principal faster while potentially saving thousands in interest payments. The private student loan market has been growing in the past few years with new ways to refinance.

Refinancing public student loans

Public (federal) student loans often go by the name Stafford loans and are issued by the Department of Education. It's possible to refinance a public student loan to a lower interest private student loan.

But, you may **not** want to refinance your public student loans. You're giving up the perks that public student loans have if you refinance, including:

- **Repayment options** – Reduced payments that are tied to your yearly income such as Income-Based Repayment (IBR) and Pay As You Earn (PAYE)
- **Deferment/Forbearance** – Nice security blankets if you find yourself out of a job for some reason
- **Public Student Loan Forgiveness** – PSLF forgives the remaining balance on your loans after you have made 120 qualifying monthly payments (ten years) under a qualifying repayment plan while working full-time for a qualifying employer.

Make a phone call to the student loan administrator at your school and ask for help. They will (hopefully) be able to walk you through your options.

Refinancing private student loans

If you have private student loans (such as from your school), it's worth contacting some of the new services that have come out in recent years to check if you qualify for a lower interest rate.

As a general rule, if you can get a lower interest rate on your *private student loans*, it's a good idea to refinance them to pay them off faster. Just like with other types of refinancing, get a lower interest rate but keep paying the same amount that was due each month before refinancing. This results in less of your payment going towards interest.

> I was able to pay off my student loans in two and a half years instead of the ten years the lender allowed because I paid extra every month.

Let's use the previous example where the original monthly payment is $383, and the new monthly payment is $371. Since you're used to paying $383 each month, keep paying that amount.

The extra $12/month prepayment will reduce your principal a little each month. It doesn't seem like much, but the loan will be paid off around *six months early*.

When you get into larger loans in the amounts of $60,000, $100,000, even $200,000 or more, the time and money savings can be significant.

It takes discipline.

Automating your payments will avoid the temptation to spend the extra you would have in your bank account each month.

Several lenders offer student loan refinancing. Make sure to comparison shop. It's so easy to compare, yet people forget to do it or don't bother doing it. You might think the biggest lenders will give you the best rates, but that's not always true:

> *I refinanced my private loans but NOT with Sofi. They denied me, and when I applied I had a 778 FICO score and no other debts! Good news is that I was able to refinance with CommonBond (Firstmark) for 7.48 percent, which is still high, but lower than what I would've been paying otherwise. I only refinanced the highest loans (about $35k).*
>
> *-Felicia, age 29, Scott Alan Turner Show listener*

Also call up a local credit union or local bank to see what offers they have. Here is a list of lenders offering student loan refinancing, in alphabetical order:

- CommonBond
- Credible
- Earnest
- LendKey
- LendEDU
- SoFi

Shopping around for student loan refinancing has never been easier. In just a few minutes you can save hundreds of dollars each month and thousands of dollars over the lifetime of a loan.

Real Debt Help

Since this book is about saving money and not a get-out-of-debt plan, we've included a resource if someone is seeking a proven plan that can change their life. Find out more at scottalanturner.com/debthelp

Saving Steps

- Speak with a legit credit counselor if you need some budgeting help
- Check out the refinancing options so more of your money can pay down principal faster
- Visit our website to learn more about become debt-free as quickly as possible

Let's turn the page now and discover how to get some discounts on stuff you're already buying.

5

Shopping

If you're a bit like me, you shop. You might shop a little or a lot, but you shop. And since everyone shops and everyone would like to have more money, it makes sense to save money when you buy stuff if it's easy to do, right? In this section you'll discover a few tricks for saving, uncover some deals at Amazon, and learn about one of the greatest money wasters hardly anyone knows about.

Money-Saving Apps

By downloading some apps that help you save money, you'll make saving much easier.

Earny

Stores change their prices all the time. Earny is a free online tool that checks your purchases to find you money when prices drop. If you buy something and it goes on sale later,

Earny *effortlessly* works by refunding you the difference. That's free money!

Retail Me Not

Get discounts with coupons and promo codes for thousands of online stores with RetailMeNot. Save offline with in-store and printable coupons!

Save Money at Amazon

Here are the best and easiest ways to save money at Amazon.

1. Discounted Amazon Gift Cards

Finding discounted Amazon gift cards can be a bit challenging, but sometimes you can score a deal.

If you're in need (or want) of something, buying discounted gift cards can save you big bucks. If you're an Amazon shopper there are several places to buy discounted Amazon gift cards:

1. Gift Card Granny is one site where you can buy Amazon gift cards at a discount. Gift Card Granny doesn't sell the cards directly but instead matches buyers and sellers.
2. Raise is another website where you can buy and sell discounted gift cards. Most of the cards I found were for 1 percent off, and the card had a value of $25.00. That's not worth the hassle. You have to stay on it to snag a good deal on Raise.

3. If one of the other sites doesn't work out, try eBay. Once again you'll have to keep track of the auction prices and how much the shipping charges are going to cost you.

2. Amazon Outlet

As the world's largest online retailer, Amazon offers loads of amazing discounts and services. You can also find great deals at Amazon's virtual outlet store on overstock items, clearance items, and markdowns.

Like with a traditional outlet store, Amazon Outlet offers deep discounts on popular, yet expensive, items.

You can score big discounts on anything from big screen TVs to tablets to clothing to furniture. Search for a specific item or browse a category (e.g., fashion) for markdowns of a specific amount (e.g., 50–80 percent off). Before you buy new from Amazon, head over to Amazon Outlet and you may save even more!

The best way to get a great deal is to comparison shop. Check out sites like Overstock too.

3. Trade-in

Using the Amazon Trade-In program, you can send items such as textbooks, electronics, video games, DVDs, and more to a third-party merchant in exchange for an Amazon gift card. Hundreds of thousands of items are eligible for exchange. The process is easy and convenient, offers are immediate, and shipping is free.

You don't get cash. Since you can buy almost anything on Amazon, a gift card is second best to cash.

There are also other sites like **BookScouter** to help you sell textbooks and used books. Make sure to compare prices to get the most for your used stuff.

4. Subscribe and Save

For everyday items, save money using Amazon's Subscribe and Save feature.

This program has been around for a while, though many Amazon shoppers haven't been aware of it. Subscribe and Save sends out shipments of the items you need on a regular basis at a discounted price. For example, Amazon Prime members save 20 percent on diaper subscriptions and more. People without Prime can also get discounts up to 15 percent. You get extra savings on eligible subscriptions when you subscribe to five or more products at one address on your monthly delivery day.

You can shop Amazon's Subscribe and Save section to see all of the products they have to offer. Each product page identifies its discount. From diapers to soap to pet treats, you can subscribe to thousands of everyday products from Amazon and Amazon Marketplace.

Set up what you want and choose your delivery frequency. **Shipping is free!** Amazon will send you a reminder before each order ships. You can skip a delivery when necessary and cancel your subscription at any time.

5. Wait and Save

Amazon prices many items a little higher than other stores. When you need an item immediately, Amazon makes a little more money. You might be willing to pay a couple of extra bucks because you want to get it now.

But Amazon is aware I'll probably also buy stuff from them I don't need right away, so Amazon's lowest price is usually lower than any other website or store.

Here is how you can save money. When you want an item that you don't need immediately, place the item in your cart. Don't buy it yet! Leave it in your shopping cart for up to two weeks and monitor the price. Over time, you can see the lows and highs of the prices. Buy items when you feel prices are at their historic "lows." Depending on the items you're buying, savings can be a few dollars into the hundreds of dollars.

This is a hit-or-miss strategy, but it has worked several times for me. You won't lose money so try it!

6. Get Today's Deals

When you're looking for Amazon bargains and deals, visit Amazon's Today's Deals pages. The Deal of the Day features hand-picked daily deals with low prices on:

- popular electronics
- tools
- things for your kitchen and home
- sporting goods
- plenty of other items

Every day you will see Lightning Deals displaying limited-time deals at great prices. These deals usually last for four hours. Make sure you buy quickly because these deals go away fast.

The Gold Box Deals showcase one item that Amazon offers an extra discount on every day.

And when Friday comes around, there is the Friday Sale, which offers discounts on over a hundred items for just one day.

When it's crunch time, and you need a last-minute gift for your significant other, a family member, a friend, or a co-worker, visit Today's Deals for a bargain. You may find a deal for yourself too!

7. Price Guarantee (TVs only)

Currently, Amazon's price guarantee will price match eligible purchases of televisions with select other retailers. **Amazon doesn't offer price matching on any other items.**

Amazon's price change policy has changed several times over the years. At one point the company allowed price refunds for thirty days after your purchase but the policy has changed to just seven days.

Before you buy that new big screen from Amazon, use the Consumer Reports TV Buying Guide to find the best model for your spending plan.

8. Family Savings

Moms are big business for retailers. The cost of diapers adds up quickly. You can save on diapers using Amazon Family.

Amazon Family provides Prime members exclusive family-oriented offers, coupons, and age-based recommendations. You can get 20 percent off diaper subscriptions and a 15 percent discount when you complete a baby registry.

Amazon Family is free for all Prime members. Simply create a child profile during signup to begin. After your free trial, Amazon Prime is just $119/year.

9. Student Discount

College kids need a break too.

For online student shoppers, Amazon offers a free trial of Amazon Prime for six months.

Under the free trial, students receive free two-day shipping, exclusive deals and promotions, and unlimited photo storage. The student fee includes extra perks such as unlimited instant streaming of movies, TV shows, and music.

After the free (limited) six-month trial period, Amazon Student costs $78 per year. Verified students (you have to have a .edu email address) are eligible for four years or until graduation, whichever comes first.

10. Amazon Store Card

You can earn 5 percent back with the Amazon Prime Store Card.

There is no annual fee.

If you use Amazon frequently, saving 5 percent on stuff you're already going to buy is a no-brainer.

> We use the Amazon store card exclusively for our Amazon purchases. It's the default card in our profile and I love getting 5 percent back on what we already planned to spend. - Scott

Cancel Unused Memberships

Grab your credit card and bank statements and see what monthly subscriptions you're paying for that you don't *need or want* anymore.

The worst subscriptions are ones where there are cheaper alternatives. **If** you've signed up to get **socks or razor blades** mailed to you each month, you could be saving more money.

Ask yourself these questions to determine if it's something you should cancel or not:

- Have I used this in the past three months?
- Do I plan on using this in the next three months?

If the answer is **No**, *cancel it*. If the answer is **Maybe**, *cancel it*. You won't miss it.

Mystery Shopping

A friend would occasionally ask my wife to join her for lunch, and she'd pick up the tab because she was secretly reviewing the restaurant as a mystery shopper. They had some very good lunches, so my wife decided to become a mystery shopper herself. I even got to go out with her on a few shops to try out restaurants.

I'll help you separate fact from fiction when it comes to getting your free lunch.

What is mystery shopping?

Stores and restaurants hire mystery-shopping companies to send in shoppers to evaluate service. When a customer is not served well in today's social media environment, they can easily share with hundreds of others about their bad experience. Retailers want independent and impartial feedback about service and products from someone paying close attention. Mystery shopping is another way for retailers to make sure training for employees is effective.

Myth: Mystery shopping makes you money

Truth: You exchange your time for free stuff

People think they can become a mystery shopper and make money in their free time.

I think a more accurate description is that you eat at no cost in exchange for your time.

My wife has mystery shopped several lunches and dinners with me, friends, or family, and it almost always costs about the amount she is allowed to get reimbursed.

For example, a mystery-shopping company might pay a reimbursement amount of $40 for two people to each lunch, plus a $5 payment.

So if two people order the food and drinks required in the shop event, the bill will likely be about $40. You only get reimbursed the amount you spend up to the limit plus the payment.

- If she spent $38 on lunch, she would be paid $38 plus $5.
- If she spent $50 on lunch, she would be reimbursed the full $40 plus $5, but wouldn't get paid the whole $50.

This isn't most people's idea of making money. But you do get the food and time with your guest.

For us, we could save a lot of money on entertainment spending and have a great time eating out three to four times a month.

Myth: Mystery shopping is easy

Truth: It requires attention to details

Mystery shopping involves reading a set of requirements and paying attention to details. Before doing a "shop," shoppers have to review what is required.

For example:

- what food needs to be ordered
- what details are important to know
- whether reservations are needed

Shoppers get a very extensive questionnaire from the place they are about to shop. There may be 50 to 100 questions to answer, along with comments and photos to take. Shoppers need to review the questionnaire a few times before going to the location so the questions are fresh in their mind. While at the event, shoppers might need to note the time, take photos, or remember a few names. Get the guest to help, if necessary.

After getting home, shoppers must quickly work on the questionnaire while the details are fresh. The questionnaires often take about an hour to fill out if you do it right. But if someone is getting $25 to $60 for a meal with a friend, it's a fair trade for a bit over an hour of time. Plus the better the report, the more likely the shopper will get hired again for more shopping.

Myth: Mystery shopping is a scam

Truth: You have to work with reputable companies only

Some people can get tricked into thinking they are working as a mystery shopper when in fact they are not. My wife was referred to a company by a friend and had to fill out a lengthy application to join the company.

Mystery-shopping companies are going to make you apply; they are not going to email you out of the blue.

Legitimate companies will not ask you to do check cashing or money transfers at Western Union or MoneyGram, etc.

A good place to start looking for mystery-shopping work is at these two legitimate websites:

- Mystery Shoppers America
- Mystery Shoppers Providers Association

Mystery shopping is fun and not too hard! Check out these websites and start eating or shopping for free!

Cash for Old Electronics

Most of us have a junk drawer full of old or outdated gadgets that we're never going to use again. If you have lots of old electronics equipment lying around, a DVD collection that you never watch, or old cellphones, you can get some quick cash. With the easy-to-use Decluttr app you simply:

1. Scan the barcode of your old CDs, DVDs, phones, games, books, tablets and more
2. Get an instant offer for your stuff
3. Mail in your stuff
4. Get fast next-day payments when your items are received

How cool is that? You can clean out your closet and get paid.

Get cash for your unwanted stuff now

Free Samples

Most personal hygiene products have high costs from the expensive marketing. Because of this, the extremely competitive nature of the hygiene aisle in your local grocery store provides you with opportunities to get your favorite products at lower costs.

If you want to get personal hygiene products for free, you'll probably have to buy brands you normally don't. You'll also have to learn how to act quickly because most of these deals don't last very long.

Start matching coupons up with sales in your local grocery store or pharmacy. Keep an eye out for free offers from manufacturers. Here are a few links to get you started.

Hunt4Freebies (Health and Hygiene Section) – This is a blog that constantly updates with free product samples, free grocery coupons, and free hygiene products that will get mailed directly to your door.

Cuckoo for Coupons – Weekly Coupon Matchup – This blog tells where to get the coupons for products that can be acquired on the cheap (or free). You can get personal hygiene products for free or at a reduced cost.

The Balance Free Samples by Mail – Some of the stuff you can get on this page is unbelievable! There are free magazines, food, and a ton of free hygiene products.

Cancel and Avoid Extended Warranties

Over your lifetime, if you never bought an extended warranty, the total money you saved would be way more than you have to pay for all of the stuff that breaks. This includes:

- electronics
- computers
- furniture
- carpets
- appliances

According to Consumer Reports, TVs fail 3 percent of the time in the first four years of ownership. It doesn't make sense to buy an expensive warranty when the chance of it failing are so small.

> Extended warranties have massive costs and are terrible purchases. If you get an offer in the mail for one, or to extend one on an existing purchase, throw it in the trash!

Most of the products that you buy already have a manufacturer's warranty, so why would you spend extra to get an extended warranty? Plus many credit cards offer to double or add an additional year to the manufacturer's warranty.

In every study by Consumer Reports, whether it's an automobile extended warranty or a TV extended warranty, they end up being a bad deal for you.

When you buy a product, instead of buying the extended warranty, save your money. Then if it breaks, you pay for it out of pocket. It's kind of like *self-insurance.* I haven't bought an extended warranty in over fifteen years. They are a bad deal for your wallet, and a golden goose for the companies that sell them. Unfortunately, companies use fear to sell these things to unknowing customers.

If you bought an extended warranty recently, see if you can get your money back.

Saving Steps

- Install the free apps that can give you discounts
- Sell your junk and unwanted stuff to get cash in your pocket
- Never buy an extended warranty again

Renters and homeowners – keep reading for quick ways to save money around the house.

6

Housing and Home Maintenance

This section looks at the most common ways to save money for both **homeowners** *and* **renters**.

Americans spend on average $2,000 per year on utilities,[9] $1,228 on home insurance,[10] and another $2,000 for upkeep.[11]

At over $5,000 per year—not even including a mortgage! – this adds up quickly. And so can the savings!

Home Insurance

A deductible is what is paid out of pocket when a claim is made against an insurance policy. For example, let's say you have a policy with a $500 deductible and there is a hail storm that requires the roof be replaced for $8,000. You would need to pay $500 out of pocket for the $8,000 roof. Insurance would pay the rest.

Most people go with the lowest deductible possible when getting home insurance. But if you raise the deductible to $2,000 or $2,500, your insurance premiums will go down, saving you money.

On average, if you increase your deductible from $500 to $2,000, you can save 16 percent on your annual home insurance.

North Carolina residents, for example, save on average 25 percent when increasing a home deductible from $500 to $1,000.

> Before you increase your deductibles, make sure you have enough money in your emergency fund to cover the cost. You want to avoid a situation where you have to charge the deductible on your credit card.

If you can afford it, take the highest deductible that your home or auto insurer will allow.

Save on Rent

There are many ways homeowners can save money, but what about if you're a renter?

Location, location, location

Long commutes are a drain on your time and finances.

As a newly minted college graduate, I made the mistake of renting an apartment in the big city of Atlanta without even having a job lined up. I got very lucky—my first job ended up being just a few miles from my apartment.

What I should have done was live in an extended stay hotel while I interviewed and found a job. I should have waited to sign a lease until I knew which part of the city I would be working in.

> *I slept on my cousin's couch in NYC while I searched for work. That's the way to do it if you can.*
>
> *Jordan - Scott Alan Turner Show listener*

Long-term lease

The longer the lease, usually the less it costs. You're saving the landlord money because they don't have to clean the apartment, replace the carpet, and paint the place as frequently.

Leases are negotiable, so always negotiate for the best rate and terms. If you know you will be at your current employer for a couple years, consider a two-year lease so the payments remain constant.

Negotiate lease renewals

Once your lease is up for renewal, the landlord usually wants to increase your rent. You have a bit of an advantage in negotiating the increase down or to zero.

If you move, the landlord has to have the place cleaned. Additionally, the apartment will be unoccupied during that time. And in their worst-case scenario, they have nobody lined up to move in. Every week or month the place remains vacant, the owner loses money.

If you like the place, try to negotiate for a lower increase or to keep your rent the same. You have power if you're willing to move out.

If you're in a hot rental market, the landlord might be willing to let you walk so they can jack up the rent price for the next tenant.

It never hurts to ask for a discount.

Move close to public transportation

One of our rental homes is within walking distance of the Dallas rail line. You can save a lot of money if you choose a location that doesn't require you to own a car or allows you to own a cheap old car you don't drive much.

When looking for apartments consider access to:

- Public transportation
- Grocery stores
- Restaurants
- Entertainment

The less you have to drive or take the train, the more you can save.

Shop around for deals

The best deal on an apartment requires considering all the options. Look outside the apartment finder magazines at the grocery store. The kind senior citizen with the basement or apartment above the garage for rent may be just what you're looking for.

Check out Craigslist and ask your co-workers and friends for recommendations.

Get a roommate

Splitting the rent with someone will always be cheaper than paying for a place of your own. In my first apartment, I paid $450/month rent with a roommate. A couple of years later I was dumping $1,000/month for a one-bedroom apartment.

I can't fault anyone for paying more to live alone. There's nothing quite like coming home and being the king or queen of the castle. If it fits your spending plan and you're ok with spending the extra to live alone, your happiness may be more important than saving money. But if not, find someone to share the rent with you.

> We have friends who have taken in people who needed a hand up, and we have done the same over the years. There are good people in the world who will let you couch surf or put you up for an extended period if you're in a bind.

Buy renters insurance

Renters insurance is the expense on this list with the lowest payback—until you need it. Most apartment complexes and landlords have insurance that protects them, not you. If an apartment catches fire or is burglarized, the dwelling is covered for the landlord. Items in the apartment are the renter's responsibility. If a renter doesn't have insurance then it's a total loss and they will not be reimbursed.

Renter's insurance will protect your purchases from theft, fire, and flood damage (depending on the policy). It's dirt cheap to get (about $125/year).

Something most people don't realize is renter's insurance also providers some level of liability protection. If a person throws a party and someone falls off the balcony or gets bit by the owner's dog, renters insurance can cover that (check the policy coverage).

Additionally, if the apartment becomes unlivable, renter's insurance can provide hotel coverage in case the renter needs to stay somewhere else temporarily.

Buy Cheap Stuff

My wife Katie picked up a like-new $1,200 Crate & Barrell kitchen table with six chairs for $400 off Craigslist. There are a lot of deals online for used stuff if you can move quickly and be the first to make an offer and pick up the item.

Buying slightly used or scuffed furniture can save a small fortune. Considering appliances and furniture are going to get scuffed, dinged, and scratched anyway, why not let someone else pay full price for new items.

Shop these places for great deals on used furniture:

- Community Facebook groups
- Freecycle
- Thrift stores

- Craigslist
- Salvation Army
- Goodwill
- LetGo

Outfit Your Kitchen to Save Money

Cooking at home can save you hundreds of dollars a month over eating out. But in order to cook at home, you need the right equipment. Certain appliances can save space, money, and time.

> I'm a huge fan of the Instapot. I picked mine up from Walmart (shop around for the best price!), and it's replaced our rice cooker, two Crock-Pots, and a yogurt maker.

The basics for a well equipped kitchen include:

- Microwave
- Ceramic sauté pan
- 8-quart stock pot
- Food processor
- Chef's knife
- Instapot

If you have those kitchen appliances, you can handle enough recipes to feed a family.

Energy Savings

Homeowners and renters have lots of ways to save money around the house. A few easy ones you probably already have heard of are:

- Installing LED bulbs (take them with you when you move out!)
- Turning off the lights when you leave
- Setting the programmable thermostat
- Air drying your laundry—yes, get a laundry rack

Additionally here are a few more energy saving tips.

Vampire appliances

According to MarketWatch, vampire appliances may waste $250 or more a year.

In total, standby energy consumption is about 10 percent of a typical electric bill.

To make it easy to ensure that electronics aren't sucking up energy when you don't need them, plug several appliances into one power strip. Then you only have to flip one switch to turn off several appliances.

For example, you could plug the TV, DVD Player, Amazon Echo, and your surround-sound speakers into the same power strip.

Stuff your fridge

This is an easy fix to save money.

Refrigerators and freezers are designed to work best when they are at least 75 percent full.

How do you keep them full if you don't have any food that needs to be kept cold? Take some empty glassware, Tupperware containers, pots, or milk jugs, fill them with water, and put them in the fridge or freezer.

The containers with water will retain the cold, reducing the need for the refrigerator to kick on.

> We had a $75 service call to figure this one out. Our fridge was not maintaining a cold temperature. The service tech showed up and said it was because we didn't have enough food in the refrigerator (maybe we were eating out too much!). Now we fill plastic jars with water to fill up the extra space. Or a case of Diet Coke.

Pull your fridge out an inch

Most refrigerators are crammed back against the wall, reducing air flow. In larger homes, the sides may be encased in cabinets, reducing air flow even more.

Refrigerators, like your outside HVAC unit, need proper airflow to function efficiently. When the refrigerator is tight against a wall, it has to work harder to keep things cool—which costs you more money.

And it doesn't matter if you're in an apartment, condo, or home. This tip applies to everyone.

Clean your refrigerator coils

Dust, lint, and **cat toys** accumulate behind the refrigerator as the unit runs and suck in air. As the dust builds up over time, the efficiency of the refrigerator decreases.

It's an easy fix. Once or twice a year, pull your refrigerator out, **unplug it**, and vacuum out the coils in the back and bottom. Newer models are sealed up better, so you might have to unscrew the back panel to get at the insides.

Cleaning the dust will allow the condenser to run more efficiently and less frequently, which saves you money. Plus, since the condenser doesn't work as hard or as much, the life of the refrigerator will be extended, saving on replacement and repair costs.

> When I look under my refrigerator, I'm always amazed to see how many cat toys have gone missing.

Switch the direction on the ceiling fan

Most people don't realize there is a reverse switch on their ceiling fan.

In the summer, we turn on our ceiling fans to save on air conditioning costs. The cooling wind-chill effect on your skin makes a room feel up to eight degrees cooler.

Doesn't it make sense to do the same thing in the winter time? Reversing the fan circulates the air around the room, making the room feel warmer and keeping you and your family more comfortable. Since your heater runs less, you reduce the cost of heating fuel.

Using ceiling fans in the winter reduces clutter and electric hazards. You won't need those space heaters and heating blankets lying around.

Childproof your walls

Contractors typically don't put insulation between an electrical outlet and the exterior siding when a home is built. Unless you have a green home or a home built in the last ten years where the builder made efficiency a priority, your outlets probably leak air, costing you money.

Leaky outlets are especially problematic in older homes.

Plastic outlet covers cost about $2 for a pack of twenty. You can plug all the outlets in your house for $4 to $6.

> The first winter in my first home, I went to plug in my vacuum. The outlet closest to my living room area was located in an exterior wall. When I put my hand down to plug in the cord—*whoosh!*—I could feel the cold air pouring in through the holes in the outlet. It didn't take long to realize all the energy being wasted. *And this was a brand-new home!*

Tax Benefits and Rebates

If you have already purchased LED lights, put in low-flow toilets, and added insulation, you may be eligible for rebates or tax credits.

Your state, city, or local utility provider may offer rebates or freebies on all kinds of energy-efficient products and solutions. Check out this link to see if you are eligible:

ENERGY STAR rebate finder

Additionally, many state and local utility companies offer home energy audits for free. Those that charge a fee may count the fee as a credit towards any work you have done in your home by the contractor. Inspectors can check your home for proper insulation, air leaks, and the energy efficiency of your heating and cooling systems.

It's worth the call to see if you can get a free inspection. Some issues they find you may be able to fix yourself to save money.

HVAC Savings

People in warmer climates can quickly see big savings in their energy bills with a few simple things to keep HVAC units running efficiently.

Remove shrubs around HVAC

Many homes put bushes around HVAC units so the unit can't be seen from the street. While it makes the home look nicer, the bushes keep the unit from operating at peak performance. HVAC units require proper air flow to operate optimally. Often the bushes intended to hide the units from plain sight end up blocking air flow.

Trimming the bushes around your HVAC unit should take about ten minutes.

HVAC maintenance

Changing out your air filters is something every homeowner can do themselves. It's cheap, easy, reduces energy use, and will prolong the life of your system.

One thing most homeowners don't do—and should do—is get their system serviced by a professional at least once a year.

HVAC units will break, and they will need to be replaced at some point. The longer you can keep them running, the more money you will save.

Check windows for broken seals

Windows can have a big impact on a homeowner's gas and electricity costs. Newer energy-efficient windows have a gas (argon) between the panes to increase energy efficiency.

This tip is huge because windows are one of the biggest sources of heat gain in the summertime.

If you see condensation or fog on your window, it means your window seal is broken, and the argon gas between the panes has escaped.

Most manufacturers have warranties, and you may be able to get free replacement windows.

> When I go running through the neighborhood, I sometimes look at people's windows to see if they have broken air leaks. Guess what? They do. I can spot them from the street. My house is several years old, and I've already had ten windows replaced. Every time, the windows are free—I pay only for the labor. While I would not buy replacement gas-filled windows just for energy efficiency, if I can get a free window replacement, I'm going to.

Replace your door sweeps

Door seals wear down over time, but rarely if ever do we look under our doors to see if there is a gap between the bottom of the door and the floor.

If you don't want to replace the door sweep, considering putting a rolled-up towel or a draft stopper next to the door to stop the drafts.

Outside the House

Do you pay someone in your neighborhood to mow your lawn or to perform maintenance on your home? Consider taking the do-it-yourself approach on many of these tasks to see if you can save money.

The best thing about YouTube is that other homeowners have published relatively easy solutions to problems that might cost you hundreds of dollars if you have a professional come to your home and diagnose.

Always check online for solutions to your home maintenance problems and only contract a licensed professional when it is necessary.

If you are a renter, some of these maintenance tasks may fall on your landlord. Most landlords are flexible. If you offer to fix the problem for them, they may reduce the rent by the cost you paid.

You could also take the same approach if you rent a house or condo. Your landlord could be responsible for mowing the grass. If you can borrow or buy a lawnmower, call your landlord and ask for a rent reduction in return for you providing the lawn care for the property. It doesn't hurt to ask!

Negotiate your lawn care

If you want a professional to take care of the yard and you use a lawn care service, call around and get several quotes for service. It's a competitive business, and the prices can vary by $10-$15 per visit. That can add up to hundreds of dollars per year for the same service.

If you are happy with your current service, call them and ask for a discount for being a loyal customer.

You: I'm looking to cut some of my expenses, and my lawn care is on the list. Can you give me a better rate?

Them: Hold on, let me check.

You will either get a better offer or you won't. If you're happy with the company, at least you tried. If you're not loyal to them, call around and find someone that will beat your current price.

DIY home services

Who doesn't love a nice green lawn free of weeds? Yearly fertilization service can cost $300/year and up for six to eight treatments.

Google the following: '*YOUR COUNTY extension office lawn fertilization*'

What you're looking for is a web page or PDF with some information on when to fertilize in your area and how much fertilization and weed control you need to apply.

> TIP – Don't buy fertilizer/weed control from your local home improvement store. These locations sell generic products that are not specific to your region. You can find the good stuff at tractor supply shops. Lesco is a commercial brand I prefer (you can find it at Home Depot sometimes).

DIY pest control

DoYourOwnPestControl.com is a website that provides information on preventive treatment, emergency treatment, application rates, and other information. You can spend $75 to $100 for a sprayer and a couple of bottles of pest control that will last you for years.

Compare that to spending $250/year to have a professional spray around your home.

Check sprinklers/change the schedule

Lawnmowers, bad drivers, aging sprinkler systems—they can all result in sprinkler heads breaking.

When spring arrives, and you turn your sprinkler system back on, run a test of the system and check each sprinkler head to make sure it's working right.

Another big water-wasting culprit is overwatering. You would be shocked, but landscapers, installers, and home builders are lousy at knowing how often you should water your lawn and for how long. Watering times can depend on:

- type of grass
- age of the lawn (new installs require more water)
- shaded versus sunny areas
- types of plants and shrubs
- time of the year
- rainfall

Doing thirty minutes of online research at your local county extension office's website can help you figure out how long each watering zone should run and how many days per week.

Install a separate water meter for irrigation

The largest expense of a water bill is for sewer treatment. For every 1,000 gallons of water going into your home, the water district will charge you to clean up the 1,000 gallons when it exits your home.

For most people, their biggest water usage comes from watering their lawn. But you shouldn't pay to have the water treated if it never leaves your property! A separate irrigation meter solves that problem.

A phone call to your water utility provider will let you know how much a separate meter will cost to install. Costs vary wildly by location.

In my first home in Atlanta, Georgia, a secondary irrigation meter cost $300. It paid for itself the first summer. In my current home in Dallas, Texas, a secondary meter is $2,500. The payback on it would probably be five to ten years. Instead, I opted to xeriscape my yard and rip out 80 percent of the grass. No watering required!

Saving Steps

- Call your home insurer and raise the deductible on your insurance
- Find all the ways you can save on utility bills around the house
- Renegotiate any services you use or consider some DIY alternatives

We've come a long way! Now that your house is in order, we need to look at health savings because even being perfectly healthy is expensive.

7

Health and Wellness

If you haven't noticed, healthcare costs are skyrocketing. My family of four spends about $10,000 per year on health insurance and doctor's visits. And we're very healthy! Anything I can do to trim the health category of our spending interests me.

Yes, you can even save money on your body, and there are a couple quick ways to do it! We'll start with life insurance, because what most people have been sold is an overpriced, inferior product where a better, cheaper solution exists.

Life Insurance

Most people are terribly underinsured when it comes to life insurance. An employer policy might provide two times an employee's salary. That's not enough coverage to make sure a family is taken care of if tragedy strikes. While a good life insurance policy is an investment in security, a bad life insurance policy can be a financial burden.

Here's the most important thing to know before reading this section:

> Never cancel an existing policy until you have a new policy in place.

The two most common types of life insurance are term life insurance and whole life insurance. Term insurance is in place for a specific term (5/10/20 years) and whole life requires paying premiums your whole life. That makes it easy to remember. Whole life is also called *permanent* insurance, since it covers the insured until they die.

The purpose of insurance is to provide financial support for a family if someone dies. The more coverage, the better. What a family should be looking to cover is the cost of college education, paying off the mortgage, and providing some retirement funds in the case of a loss of income.

Take, for example, a newly married couple who expect to have a family. A twenty-five-year term policy for $1 million would cover the family for twenty-five years. The term would likely be enough to make sure college tuition was paid and the mortgage could be paid off, if the person insured died before the twenty-five-year coverage ended.

Avoid whole life insurance

The only people that like whole life insurance are the people that sell the policies and make huge commissions. You won't find one personal finance expert who will tell you to buy it. Doesn't that speak volumes about what a horrible product whole life insurance is?

There are a bunch of reasons salespeople try to convince others about the benefits of whole life insurance: it includes an investment component, you can borrow against the built-up cash, and there are tax advantages.

Well, you can have those things for a fraction of the cost by going with a term life policy and saving the outrageous premium costs of whole life on your own.

The life insurance industry's big secret is that almost 90 percent of policies lapse.[12] People pay big up-front commissions for whole life insurance, and 90 percent of them end the policies before they ever collect the death benefit.

If someone sold you on whole life, it's time to find a different salesperson to explain term life insurance to you. Term life insurance is about 1/20th of the cost for ten times the protection,

making it more likely you will keep the coverage to make sure your family is protected.

If you switch from whole life to term and invest the difference, you'll come out much better in the long run.

If you have an existing whole life policy, contact evaluatelifeinsurance.org for an independent, third-party, unbiased opinion on whether you should cancel or keep your existing policy. *Disclosure: I have no affiliation with this company and receive no compensation for referring people to them.*

Cancel life insurance for children

Life insurance is for the protection of financial assets, such as if a primary breadwinner in the family is lost. Children are not financial assets. Parents get sucked into buying life insurance for their children because salespeople tell them it's what every loving parent would do. *It's a waste of money.* The likelihood of a child dying is minimal, and children are not a source of income (which is what life insurance protects). These products are huge profit centers for insurance companies. Don't play their game.

I have kids. I love my kids (twin five-year-olds). I've never had insurance policies on them and never will.

People aren't *bad* parents if they don't buy life insurance on their kids. They are *smart* parents.

Cheaper Prescription Drugs

Stop paying too much for your prescriptions! If you take any medication on a regular basis, that can be a big expense. It can cost a lot to stay healthy, especially for seniors or people with medical conditions.

Drug prices vary wildly by pharmacy, so comparison shopping is important. The GoodRx app collects prices and discounts from over 60,000 US pharmacies so you can save money.

GoodRx also has coupons that you can use to lower your cost on prescriptions. You can print free coupons or have coupons sent to your phone by email or text message. You could save up to 80 percent when you show the coupon to your pharmacist.

Generic drugs are another cost-saving measure. Ten years ago, just under 50 percent of drugs sold were generics. Generics now account for 80 percent of all prescriptions.

A lot of the grocery stores, big box retailers, and online pharmacies offer $4 generics. Most of these places provide a thirty-day supply for select drugs. Sometimes you can find a ninety-day supply for $10. Next time you're at the doctor or you go into the 24-hour emergency clinic, ask if there's drug that would work for you and save you some money. It doesn't hurt to ask.

Cancel Unused Gym Memberships

> I was talking to someone who paid for a monthly gym membership, hadn't been there in three months, and said she should go back again soon.

While your gym membership might be cheap—$30/month—that's $360/year you're paying for not using something. If you haven't been to the gym in a couple of months, save yourself the money and ditch the membership.

Or at least freeze it

If you think you'll be going back "sometime," meet with the gym manager and ask to have a freeze put on your membership. Most gyms will allow you to put a 90- to 120-day freeze. It doesn't cancel it, but it stops the monthly bills. Then after your freeze ends you can decide if you want to keep the membership or not.

Dispute Your Medical Bills

If you have had an emergency and are left with a huge pile of medical bills, negotiate them to save money.

Call the hospital or doctor and ask to speak with the billing department. Tell them you are unable to pay the balance (assuming you can't) and explain your situation. Ask them what they can do to lower the total.

If you don't get anywhere, consider working with a professional bill negotiator to save you big bucks. Check out CoPatient.

Sign Up for an HSA

A health savings account (HSA) lets you put money away for medical expenses not covered by your insurance. Every dollar you contribute reduces your taxable income by that amount.

HSA holders can choose to save up to $3,500 for an individual and $7,000 for a family (HSA holders fifty-five and older get to save an extra $1,000.) These contributions are 100 percent tax deductible from gross income.

Given the out-of-pocket costs we're all paying for healthcare nowadays, an HSA is worth participating in either through your employer or by signing up for a plan on your own (depending on your insurance). You can save hundreds of dollars per year on your taxes.

Ask your employer if there is an HSA you can participate in.

Saving Steps

- Get an audit of your life insurance to make sure you're not overpaying for under-coverage
- Use discount prescription services to save on prescriptions
- Start using an HSA if you have access to one

By now you're probably getting a little hungry! Good, because next up we're going to save money on food.

8

Groceries

American households spend about $7,000 a year, on average, on food alone. High income households spend about $12,000 per year on average.

Groceries are one of the biggest cost categories in most families' spending.

This is average spending, which means that it is not a fixed cost. It can be reduced just as we cut our transportation expenses by using public transportation or driving cheaper cars. So, instead of aiming to spend the national average of your income group, you can come up with your own unique food spending plan.

Before You Shop

Easiest way to save

The number one decision you make that will save you money on your groceries is **where you shop**.

Overall you will find the best prices on groceries at Walmart.

There is no reason to buy your toilet paper at Whole Foods. Whole Foods—also known as Whole Paycheck—has some great food. The great food also comes with great prices. And by great I mean high.

If you do all of your shopping at a single store all the time, you're missing out on some savings. I usually buy from:

- Costco (meat, paper products)
- Walmart (produce, dry and canned goods)
- and yes, even occasionally Whole Foods (bulk-container foods)

You can also check out nontraditional grocery stores. Take Aldi and Dollar Tree for example. They have smaller, cheaper selections. They don't have as many locations but are worth investigating.

By taking the time to learn where you can get the best prices on certain products, you can easily add to your savings.

Make a shopping list

Having a shopping list is the second biggest way to save on groceries. It gives you a plan to buy what you want and ignore the things in the store you don't.

> I've found I will overspend by up to 25 percent if I show up at the supermarket without a list. The cart gets filled with all kinds of snacks, produce, etc., that we don't need or hadn't planned on eating.

Take fifteen to twenty minutes *before* you leave for the grocery store (or do it the night before) and write down what you need to buy. Once you hit the store, you will be on a mission to get your items checked off and get out. No dilly-dallying, messing around, and wasting money.

Use the cash envelope system

Overspending is easy when you whip out the plastic at the checkout counter. When you use the cash envelope system and pay with cash for your groceries, you can only spend what you have in cash.

The cash envelope system (or envelope system) uses a spending plan to prevent overspending. For example if a person decides to spend $400 on groceries for the month and they get paid twice per month, on payday they would withdraw $200 from the ATM machine. That cash goes in an envelope labeled "groceries." When it's time to grocery shop, the $200 in cash is what's available to spend on groceries until the next payday.

The biggest benefit of the cash envelope system and planning ahead of time where your money will go (instead of wondering where it went), is it will make you a better spender. It hurts more to spend cash (compared to the ease of swiping a plastic credit card), and people naturally focus on making better spending choices.

Plus, having a spending limit (there's only so much cash in the envelope!) forces you to make better choices with the limited amount. It's easy to go to a grocery store with no plan or list, load up the grocery cart, and pay whatever the total is. But you end up with more money over time (a lot more!) by making a shopping list and sticking to what you've decided to spend.

> The envelope system helps you make wiser choices on what to buy. It's been critical in helping me and Katie not overspend and build wealth.

Clip coupons

Extreme couponing is just that—extreme. I've watched episodes of that show where people have walked out of grocery stores with $700 worth of products and paid $3.00 at the cash register. The people on those shows typically spend thirty to forty hours per week clipping and organizing coupons. *It was almost a job.*

But you don't have to go to that extreme to save some money on groceries. Coupons are an easy way to save money.

Buy two or three copies of the Sunday paper to get started and cut out all the coupons for the stuff you think you'll want.

Visit CouponMom.com to save time on finding deals. And if you have a favorite product, send a quick email to the manufacturer telling them you like their product and ask them if they have any coupons. You may be surprised when they send you some.

Consider memberships

Wholesale memberships like Costco, when used appropriately, can lead to tremendous cost savings. The savings you'd get on buying a new mattress alone (my favorite example) would cover the cost of your membership, and that's before any other savings you'd pick up all year.

If your community has a local co-op, take a look at what membership will give you. Many co-ops support local farmers and merchants, which means you'll have direct access to cheaper in-season produce. Many co-ops will also let you make bulk orders at prices slightly above wholesale.

Thrive Market is an online retailer that gets a lot of buzz for offering great prices on healthy and organic foods shipped right to you. There's a membership fee for Thrive, but many members say it's absolutely worth it.

At the Store

Compare prices by weight

People can be fooled into thinking a bigger bag or box is cheaper. Not always so. To be a savvy shopper, you must look at the price per unit. This strategy works for everything from food to cat litter.

On the store label (where you see a price), in smaller print is typically the price per unit. The units are usually ounces or grams. The lower the per-unit price, the lower the cost.

Here's an example for a 28-ounce can of tomatoes versus a 14-ounce can of tomatoes. Let's say the 28-ounce can costs $1.49 and the 14-ounce can is on sale for $0.50.

The 28 oz can costs $0.053 cents per ounce. ($1.49/28)
The 14 oz can costs $0.035 cents per ounce. ($0.50/14)

The larger 28-ounce can is *more expensive* per ounce. It's pretty easy to compare the per-unit price for different sizes when they are side-by-side in the store. Take the five seconds to do it and you can save money easily.

It's important, because sometimes smaller cans and packages are cheaper than the bigger ones when you look at per-unit price. The savings really add up when you figure in the thousands of dollars being spent on groceries each year for the average family. This quick comparison could easily save hundreds of dollars.

> Here's one of the biggest bad deals for you: smaller 8 oz cans of Coke cost twice as much per ounce as 12 oz cans of Coke. You're better off buying 12 oz cans and dumping the extra down the drain.

Avoid prepackaged items

Any time you walk into a grocery store and purchase packed items like fruit snacks, meals in a bag, frozen grilled vegetables, chips, or even pre-sliced produce, you're paying a premium on them.

Processed and packaged food items cost more because of the work done on them. I'm no lover of kitchen chores but I have come to realize that peeling potatoes at home will save you a lot, even though it is time consuming. Bottom line; it's worth the effort. If you have kids, *put them to work.*

Reduce meat consumption

There are people that think that in order for a meal to have enough protein, it must have meat. Meat is the most expensive way to get a protein fix.

An average adult requires approximately seventy-five grams of protein each day. A meal of rice and beans will give you the complete amount of protein you need at virtually no cost. Eggs are another tasty and economical way of getting the protein you need, as they have the highest quality of complete protein.

For example, compare one dozen eggs that cost $2.00 to one pound of ground beef which costs $4.99. Three eggs and 4 oz. of ground beef have about the same amount of protein. Both can make four servings, but the eggs cost much less.

Skip bottled water

Clean water is a luxury that all of us take for granted. There was an article written several years ago about how bottled water can cost you more than gas. In fact, the average family spends $250 per year on bottled water, when the stuff that comes out of the tap (almost free!) is just as good.[13]

If you are spending money on bottled water—**STOP!**

A recent survey said that a majority of people who preferred bottled water did so for health reasons. This reasoning contrasts with experts who suggest that the health differences between bottled and tap are *negligible*.

- If water purity is a concern, a good alternative would be to buy a Brita filter for your faucet, saving hundreds of dollars per year.[14]
- For those serious about water filtration, the Berkey Water Filtration System is a high-end solution for purified water.
- Or you could ditch bottled water altogether and buy a Nalgene bottle and simply fill it up using tap water.

Use a cash-back credit card

If you're not into using a cash envelope system, make sure you use a credit card that offers you the most back on your grocery purchases.

American Express Blue Cash Preferred Card offers 6 percent cash back on grocery purchases, up to $6,000 annually. For an average family, this card could provide $240 in savings. Make sure any annual card fees don't offset the savings.

The Costco Anywhere Visa card gives 2 percent cash back on all Costco purchases. If you're already shopping at Costco to save on bulk groceries, this could save another 2 percent.

Don't shop hungry. Or with your kids.

You've heard this phrase: *My eyes were bigger than my stomach.* When you shop hungry, you buy more. Period. And you're more likely to buy snacks and other items you haven't built into your spending plan.

You know what else makes you buy things you don't need? Bringing your kids to the store. They don't understand grocery lists or spending plans. They want the Milky Way candy bars. The Oreos. The supersize box of Franken Berry cereal. And they'll state their preferences loudly. You might find yourself giving in to make them happy.

Shopping alone helps you stick to your list and your spending plan.

Buy store brands

Consumer Reports did some research[15] on food, comparing name brands to store brands.

30 percent - The percent of store-brand foods that were cheaper than name brands.
60 percent - The percent of store-brand foods that tasted as good as or better than the name brand.

The name-brand premium is largely the result of advertising and promotional costs that are passed on to consumers.

Hey, if you're in love with Cheerios, the next time you're at the store just try the generic Toasty O's or Honest O's and see what you think. You might be surprised to find they taste better or exactly the same. And you'll save money.

Buy in bulk

You don't have to have a warehouse club membership to buy in bulk. I've found some of the best deals at a little produce market near my house on bulk items like oatmeal, nuts, and trail mix. You can even get deals on bulk items at Whole Foods. Just check what they have on sale for the week.

I bought steel cut oats from the produce market on sale for $1/pound. Walmart was selling cans for $2/pound, or twice as much.

And don't forget Amazon, which can be cheaper than warehouse clubs. If you're looking for cheap staple foods in bulk, check them out. Amazon has a wide selection of packaged goods. Prices can vary, so comparison shopping is a good idea when buying in bulk.

At Home

Eat what you have

Most families could save **$2,300 a year** just by not wasting food.

The Natural Resources Defense Council (NRDC) reported recently **we are throwing away 40 percent of our food each year!**[16] We lose money on leftovers at home from cooking, leftover restaurant food, and food that spoils or we just don't feel like eating (hello, spinach). It adds up to $165 billion in wasted food each year, or nearly $2,300 each year for the typical family.

We're all guilty of this. Take a look around your fridge and pantry every couple of days and commit to eating what is already in your house or what is getting ready to expire. If you're not going to eat leftovers right away, put them in the freezer for later.

Make a few things yourself

Convenience foods are expensive foods. Buying raw ingredients and cooking is not only healthier, but it's also cheaper.

You don't have to go crazy, cooking three nights a week at home to save money. Identify a few processed or packaged foods that cost a lot and see what it would take to make your own cheaper versions.

Picking a few things to occasionally cook at home will have big savings.

For example, Greek yogurt at the store is expensive—$4 a container, or $1 per serving. But the Instapot has a yogurt function where you can make your own yogurt. You can save **$219 per year** by doing this. The best part is it's as easy as dumping a gallon of milk into the pot.

Does your family like oatmeal? Buying oatmeal in bulk can cost $1 per pound, which is half the cost of packaged oats at Walmart. Again, throw it in the Instapot and you can have enough oatmeal for an entire *week of breakfasts in just 20 minutes, for only $1.*

Rebates on stuff you already bought

Check out some of the many savings apps available for shopping. One example is Ibotta, an app that is better than coupons and pays you real cash money! Ibotta offers you an excellent way to save by getting rebates. All you have to do is:

1. Create an account for free
2. Download the mobile app
3. Click on 'Rebates'

On the Rebates page, you will find a lot of hot offers. Just take photos of your receipts and get rebates. These rebates vary depending on the promotion and the product.

Save on Organics

Organic food is more popular than ever. Gallup polling reports that 45 percent of people look specifically for organic foods over conventionally raised crops and meats.

Sales of organic foods have jumped to nearly *$40 billion per year.*

- **Kroger's Simple Truth** line of organic products brings in over $1 billion per year.
- **Costco's Kirkland Signature** lineup of organic foods brings in around $3 billion.
- **Walmart's organic brands** are expanding across thousands of stores.

While Whole Foods is still the undisputed leader in organic products, the offerings from many of those large food retailers is eating into their profits, which have dropped 10 percent over the last several years.

Many people want to eat organic but think they can't afford it. But the truth is, many supermarkets have begun offering cheap, organic products. If you look around for deals and coupons, you can buy organic food even if you're on a spending plan.

The next few sections will provide ways that you can enjoy fresh, organic produce without busting your plan.

Farmers markets

Farmers markets are the best way to get fresh, organic produce from local farmers. While the prices do tend to be higher than supermarket prices, the food is fresh, chemical-free, and you are supporting local farmers. Do some quick Internet research to find markets near you.

There is a way for *low-income families* to take advantage of low-priced organic products through farmers markets. An EBT incentive program is available to families who use EBT to purchase food. The program allows users to spend $10 and receive an additional $10 free.

The EBT incentive programs are at participating farmers markets in many areas, so check around to determine if your local farmer's markets are participating.

Buy in season

Fruits and vegetables will taste better and cost less when they are in season.

For example, in the United States, it is cheaper to buy strawberries in summer when they are simple to grow in the US than in winter when they get shipped up from South America.

Do a quick Google search for in-season produce when making your recipe/shopping list. If you want summer vegetables or fruit in the winter, try the frozen section. Food frozen at peak times of year typically retain their nutrient profile.

Shop around

The problem with many of the organic supermarkets is that prices fluctuate on specific items at different times. For instance, you may go to a Walmart and find a product that is one price. Another discount organic supermarket may have the same product at a much higher or much lower price.

The reason is that some products are harder to obtain at certain times of the year. So the prices fluctuate based on this availability. However, many stores price match their competitors. If you can check prices online ahead of time, you may be able to do all your shopping at the same grocery store.

Alcohol

Here are some tips to save money on adult beverages.

Buy at the warehouse clubs

Shopping at the warehouse clubs (Sam's, Costco, BJ's) can save you money over buying at grocery stores and liquor stores. Costco's Kirkland signature brand is a great store brand compared to big name brands.

You can expect to save 20 to 30 percent on the Costco brand over name-brand alternatives.

Avoid name-brand misconceptions

The entire inspiration for this section came from a Buzzfeed video comparing name-brand liquor to Costco's store-brand liquor, Kirkland.

So how did the store brand compare to Grey Goose and Captain Morgan's?

The tasters frequently could not agree on which was better. And they were tasting *straight alcohol.* **No mixers!**

Google the Costco Liquor vs. Brand-Name Liquor blind taste test.

The bottom line is you can save some coin by buying your alcoholic beverages at Costco.

Beware of overhyped brands

It's well documented that Grey Goose increased the price of their vodka to make it appear more expensive and elite. The marketers then went to work to get consumers to believe it.

And they did!

Like Starbucks coffee, in taste test after taste test Grey Goose fails to win testers over other low-brow brands.

When people buy Grey Goose, they are paying more for marketing, not for a better product or better flavor. People can't taste the difference.

Try this at-home test: Take an empty bottle of Grey Goose, fill it with the cheapest vodka you can find, and serve it to your guests in whatever concoction you prefer.

- See if they notice any taste difference
- Ask them what they think of the vodka
- Refrain from embarrassing them when you tell them it's some generic vodka (unless they are a jerk, but that's on you)

We did this at a party we hosted once. Nobody could tell the difference.

You can choose to save money by not falling for flashy advertising. Just refill a name-brand bottle with a cheap alternative and keep it your own little secret.

Other tips

Check out corner drugstores

Sometimes you can find a deal on beer at CVS or Walgreens.

Who knew?

Try "second label'" wines

Second label wines are a cheaper version of their more expensive brothers.

> The concept of second label wines began in Bordeaux in the 18th century as a means for producers to utilize wine that was not chosen for the Chateau's first label. Rather than waste this excess wine or sell it in bulk, the second label allowed winemakers to bottle and sell this still very high-quality wine under their name and through their distribution channels.

You're getting wines that don't get as much love from the winemakers as the first label bottles.

Buy off brands

Off brands are discounted brands from the same company. It's best explained with an example:

At a restaurant, Duckhorn wine may cost you $120 a bottle.

At Costco I've seen it for $30 a bottle.

Duckhorn's lower-priced off brand is called Decoy and sells for $19.99 at Costco.

As you can see, it's a $100 difference between what a restaurant sells the higher end name-brand wine for compared to what's available at a discount store for the off brand, made at the same facility by the same wine maker.

Look for store specials

The liquor stores near me always have specials going on for certain products. When you visit a liquor store, you might as well buy something that's on sale.

Avoid monthly clubs

It's cool to get a new bottle of wine or a case of microbrew. But if you join a wine/beer-of-the-month club, you're getting pegged every month with another credit card charge.

It's cheaper to go to a store each month and seek out a deal.

Saving Steps

- Make a grocery list for next week because planning is a must for saving on groceries
- Eat or freeze the leftovers in the fridge
- Pick three easy things to make this week that would save money

Now that you have saved money on food at home, let's turn the page to save money on eating out.

9

Eating Out

Kris Ruby of New York City lost her credit card and had to borrow her dad's while waiting for a new one. When her dad looked at the bill, he found she had spent **$225 in seven days** on sushi and salads. She calculates she spends **$11,000 a year on takeout**.

Jason Saltzman tallied up the costs of eating out three times a day, and found he was spending **$1,800 a month**. That's a mortgage payment for a house.

Those are some extreme examples, but the average American family spends **$2,668 per year** ($225 a month) eating away from home.

That includes

- coffee on your way to work
- lunch away from the office

- afternoon snacks from the cafeteria or vending machine
- dinners out

The money you spend on eating out is one of the simplest spending categories to tweak to help you get out of debt, save money, and build wealth. You'll be surprised how much extra you can sock away into a Roth IRA or a fund for a shiny new car.

These are ideas on how to keep more in your wallet. Not a single thing I'm going to talk about has anything to do with buying more groceries or cooking at home. Every suggestion is based on one thing—*continuing to eat out.*

Eating Out On a Spending Plan

Katie and I *love* eating out. And we've been eating out on a spending plan since we got married in 2005. The spending plan has allowed us to come a long way since our first Valentine's Day at Chipotle.

Prioritize your spending

So you've decided you simply must have the Wednesday night pizza as part of your routine to make it through the week.

Then order the Wednesday night pizza.

Before you do, figure out where the money is going to come from. Many people just pile on more credit card debt and get stuck in the paycheck-to-paycheck cycle. It can lead to paying for the pizza over and over again for years.

If you have a working spending plan and want to eat out more, take money from other variable spending categories.

We do this all the time. Pull money from the grocery category to eat out or to throw a dinner party. Sometimes we pull from the entertainment category to buy more groceries (if it's a fancy meal).

Another option is to brown bag your lunch and put that extra towards a night out.

Make a plan

You'll have more money to eat out on Saturday if you plan your week in advance. It's easy to go through the drive-thru when you are driving home from work or picking up the kids. As we experienced recently with a $29 bill from McDonald's for five people, *even cheap fast food isn't cheap.*

And something simple like takeout Chinese can be **$12 for one person!**

It adds up fast. Do that twice a week, and you've blown through $100 for a family of four before Saturday rolls up.

Instead of eating out three times at three places you won't even remember next week, save up for one nice meal and have an experience you'll enjoy more.

Plan ahead and give some thought to where you want to eat out the most. Believe me, the meal will taste much better because of the anticipation.

Think of it like this: if you ate cookies for breakfast, lunch, and dinner, after about two weeks, you would hate cookies. If you ate cookies once every two weeks, you'd circle that date on the calendar and enjoy every last crumb.

Be content

It's fun to eat at nice restaurants and enjoy great service. But only the super rich can *afford* to spend thousands of dollars eating out every month.

And if you're getting out of debt or trying to save up for retirement or a house, spending more on eating out will only delay your **other more important goals**.

> The $10 meal really costs $13. You had to earn $13 and then pay taxes, leaving you with $10. If the $13 were invested in tax-deferred investments, it would be worth $30 in 10 years. Which doesn't seem like much, but it is if you eat out for lunch every day. Eating out adds up very quickly!

You'll need to figure out your healthy balance between saving and spending based on your goals and how long you want to take to reach them. Depriving yourself by never eating out is just as likely to lead to failure in getting out of debt as continuing to eat out.

Before You Go Out

Grab a snack

If the last time you ate before going to dinner is lunch, you're probably going to be super hungry and order too much food for dinner. I do this all the time. It's no different than going to the grocery store when you are hungry; you buy more groceries than you would otherwise.

Grab some nuts, fruit, a snack bar, or a little something around 4 p.m. to hold you over until dinnertime. Then when dinnertime rolls around you won't be tempted to order an appetizer, soup, salad, entree, dessert, and another dessert.

Another option is the pre-party. This before-dinner gathering cuts down on your restaurant check because you've already had drinks or snacks before you go out. That's a savings at the bar or restaurant.

Savings: $5–$20 per person

Kids eat free!

You can save money if you have little ones. Check out the website Kids Meal Deals to search for restaurants near you where kids eat for free.

Savings: $5 per child

Get social

Use your smartphone to check Yelp, Facebook, Twitter, or Instagram for any discounts the restaurant is offering. Sometimes you can get a discount or a free appetizer for checking yourself in with Facebook.

Savings: $5–$10 per person

Pad your stomach with H2O

Your stomach is only so big and can only hold so much. If you fill it up with water, you will feel fuller, causing you to order less and eat less when dining.

Savings: $5–$10 per person

Restaurant clubs

Check out if your favorite restaurants have an email club. If they do, sign up and you can get notices about special events, dinner specials, or maybe a free or discounted meal on your birthday.

Savings: $5–$10 per person

Loyalty cards

When I lived in Atlanta, we went to Moe's Southwestern Grill about once a week. After ten visits to Moe's, you got a free burrito.

There's no Moe's near where I live now, but there is this cupcake place that gives me a free cupcake after I buy 20. I'd rather not say how many free cupcakes I've received.

Frequent places that have loyalty programs and you could get some free meals occasionally (or free cupcakes).

Savings: $5–$10 per person

Meal deals

With Restaurant.com, you can buy gift certificates online for restaurants in your area.

You can save up to 50 percent on your bill!

Savings: 10 percent to 50 percent per bill

Be sure to check out the minimum purchase required for ordering.

Discount gift cards

I see these at Costco all the time. Buy a $100 gift card for California Pizza Kitchen for $79.99.

You just got $20 worth of free food!

What's the catch?

A research study showed $750 million on gift cards went unredeemed in 2014. They are counting on you to not use your gift card.

Savings: $10–$20 per bill

Use coupons

Every week I get that big thick packet of coupons in the mail for services I'll never use, like window washing, buying new blinds, installing a pool in my backyard.

But they always have coupons for restaurants in the area. Especially pizza places.

Savings: $3–$10 per bill

Pay with cash

You are more likely to spend more when paying with a credit card than paying with cash.

One of the most often cited studies is one conducted by Dun & Bradstreet, where the company found that people spend 12–18 percent more when using credit cards instead of cash. McDonald's reports its average ticket is $7 when people use credit cards versus $4.50 for cash.

Pulling cash out of your wallet hurts more because you see it leaving, never to come back.

Pay with cold hard cash and you will spend less.

Savings: 12–18 percent per bill

When to Eat

Lunch is less

Many places have special lunch menus with lower-priced entrees. This option also gives you a chance to try out a nicer restaurant that might otherwise be too expensive for dinner.

Savings: $10–$30 per bill

Eat with the early birds

Restaurants often have an "early bird special."

You could try eating early to get a deal. Then when it's 6 p.m. and other people are heading out to eat, you can go see a movie and enjoy an empty theater.

Savings: Beats me, I've never eaten dinner at 4 p.m.

Happy, happy, happy hour

One time a group of friends and I went to celebrity chef Stephan Pyles' restaurant before a charity ball. We got there during happy hour where they had $4 wine from the bar. That was the key though—we had to order the drinks from the bar. The same glass if we sat down at our table was $9.

So we all went to the bar and ordered two drinks each before sitting down for dinner.

Eating during happy hours—4–7 p.m. depending on the location—can give you savings on drinks and appetizers.

Savings: $5–$20 per bill

Buffets

Buffets are a sweet deal to cut your dining costs.

All-you-can-eat salad bars can be a good option too. Yes, carnivores, I know you think you won't find anything to eat and it's going to suck, but I've been to some really good salad bars that have pizza, pasta, bread, brownies, cookies, soups, stews, and more. I've never left a salad bar hungry.

Savings: $10–$20 compared to a full-service restaurant

Drinks

BYOB

If you live in a big city or the suburbs you are more likely to find a restaurant that doesn't have a liquor license and will allow you to bring your own beer and wine.

If there is an eating establishment near you that doesn't serve alcohol, call them up and ask if you can bring your own. They might say yes.

Savings: $20 per bill

Buy the glass

If you go to a place with a separate wine list:

A. It's probably an expensive restaurant

B. There probably isn't going to be a bottle of wine less than $60

C. The next cheapest bottle is probably $80

They probably have a few selections of wines by the glass in the $10–$14 range.

That's still a lot of money for a glass of wine. But compared to a bottle, you might be better off.

Savings: $5–$20 per bill

Corkage fees

Some places allow a "corkage fee" of $20. People can bring any bottle of wine they want to the restaurant and they will charge $20 to open it.

You may think $20 to pull a cork is absurd (it is), but it's a deal.

For example La Crema is a really good wine Walmart sells for $14 a bottle. In the restaurant, it might cost $50 a bottle. Buy the $14 bottle, pay a $20 corking fee, and it's $16.00 saved. The more expensive the wine, the more the savings.

Call the restaurant ahead of time and ask if they have a corkage fee. It's that simple.

Savings: $15 and up

Skip the fountain drinks

Fountain drinks are $2.50 to $3.50 per person at even a modest chain restaurant like Chili's or Macaroni Grill. If you dine out just once per week as a couple, that's $20 to $28 a month ($240-$336 per year!) on Coke, Pepsi, and iced tea.

Savings: $2–$4 per person

Water

In fine dining establishments, you always are presented with the option to buy fancy water from a bottle that has been run through some type of reverse osmosis filter to remove impurities. Or maybe it was bottled from an Alaskan glacier and has been frozen for 400 years. Sometimes even an upscale pizza place will ask you if you want fancy water.

Servers may not even give the option to drink tap water. Apparently some restaurants are not connected to the public water supply and don't have any faucets in the building. Who knew?

Don't fall prey to embarrassment and pressure to pay for expensive fancy water. Ask for tap water. In fact those are my exact words when I'm asked this question by my server: "Tap water is fine, thanks."

Fancy water and tap water—they taste the same but only one is free.

Savings: $10 per bill

Appetizers

There are several ways to save money on appetizers.

Skip the crab cakes and nachos

The appetizers coming out of restaurants these days are as big as your head. Crab cakes, nachos, chips and salsa, cheese plates—these are entire meals in themselves. An easy way to trim your dining spending is to skip the appetizers.

Savings: $6–$16 per bill

Skip the soup too

You should be offended restaurants are charging $3 to $5 for a cup of soup. You can get a can of Campbells soup at Walmart for $0.99.

And how often do you get a *really* good cup of soup at a restaurant that was worth $5? Think about it. I bet it's about 10 percent of the time.

Savings: $3–$5 per person

Eat more bread

Load up on free bread and you'll be so full you won't want an entree.

Carbs!

Savings: $5–$10 per person

Salads, the silent killers

Yes we all need our greens, but for an extra $3? Some restaurants include an add-on salad with your main dish. But it's also an add-on to your bill. Chain restaurants typically have this combo.

Savings: $2–$4 per person

Ordering

Split the check

When you go out to eat with a group of friends or family, unless you want to get stuck overpaying you absolutely must memorize the following and *always* make them the first words out of your mouth to your server:

You: Can you split the check, please?

If you don't learn and use those words, *you* are going to get stuck paying for someone else's $10 drink and $15 appetizer when all you ordered was a water and a salad—because you were smart and on a spending plan.

Since you're already smart and on a spending plan, just try it:

Server: What would you like to drink sir/miss?

You: Can you split the check, please?

I can't tell you how many times I've been stuck overpaying because of this "let's just split the check evenly" nonsense. If they order a $50 two-ounce-pour of Homer Simpson VIII fifty-year-old whiskey, you should not have to pay for it.

Split an entree

Couples have the advantage of ordering one entree and splitting it between them. Boom! You just saved at least $15 by not ordering a second entree.

Savings: $15–35 per bill

Appetizers only

Check out the menu and decide what looks more appealing to you and consider how hungry you are.

I eat at Red Lobster once every two years, and the only reason I go there is for the fried clams. It's only available as an appetizer so I place an order for two of them. That's the meal! Fried clams and cheese biscuits. Love it!

Savings: $10–$20 per person

Sharing is caring

Side items are typically hefty in size. If you are out with other people, share them.

Savings: $5–$10 per bill

Lunch for a week

If you've ever gone to the Cheesecake Factory, you've seen the menu the size of an encyclopedia. The meal portions are just as large, enough to feed a small family of five for three days, with enough left over to freeze for a later date.

Once your meal hits the table, divide it in half and immediately place half of it in a take-home box. You now have lunch for the next five days.

While this doesn't save you money on eating out, it does reduce your grocery spending because you have a lunch. If you typically eat out for lunch at work, it will save you money because you'll be sitting at your desk or in the break room eating your yummy leftovers. It beats a tuna sandwich.

Savings: $5–$10 per person

Chicken is boring (and cheap)

In the world of restaurants, the entrees with the highest profit margin are pastas and chicken, and they are also the cheapest menu items.

Steak and seafood are more expensive and have lower profit margins.

Instead of the filet or lobster tail try the grilled chicken occasionally.

Savings: $5–$10 per person

Dessert options

It annoys me dessert prices have almost doubled over the past few years at places like Applebee's from $4 to $5 to now $9 to $10. I have decided to boycott restaurant desserts because of my outrage, and I hope you will join me in avoiding high prices for lousy desserts. It took me years of thinking on this to finally come to these better options.

Dessert elsewhere

If you're in an area with a lot of dining options, go to an ice cream or cupcake shop nearby after the meal. It will definitely be cheaper.

Savings: $3–$5 per person

Dessert at home

For Valentine's Day one year, I purchased two containers of Ben & Jerry's for Katie and me to eat after we got back from dinner.

$3.98 each for my favorite ice cream at home versus $9.00 each for dessert at the restaurant.

Savings: $3–$5 per person

Check Please

I saved the biggest money saver for last because it's the most important to you having financial freedom in your life. I've shared a lot of tips that will save you some serious coin. But, you see, this next one is the biggest of the bunch.

Eating out is way more fun if you're not going into debt to do it.

I decide each month in advance how much money I'm going to spend on entertainment and eating out. I take that cash out of the bank on the first of every month and stick it in an envelope. That's it for the month—no more, no less. When I go out, I take as much cash as I think I'll need or want to spend.

If it gets to be the end of the month and the envelope is empty, I go eat a big steak and charge it to a credit card.

No, that's how you get into debt. If you don't borrow money you can't be in debt.

You don't want to be paying interest on a lasagna dinner you bought eight months ago, do you?

Does that make sense?

If I run out of entertainment money because on the second day of the month I blew it all at a fancy restaurant, well, that's it. I wear big boy pants so I have to act like a big boy in life and with money.

Savings: $50–$250 per month

Avoid Restaurant Tricks

Eating out is both fun and convenient, so how can you save money eating out when the restaurants have gamed their menus to get you to spend more?

In their bid to make more money and make themselves more popular, restaurant menu makers and consultants have come up with some sneaky tricks to make you spend more than you normally would. The things they come up with are not rocket science. It's pretty basic stuff, but we don't really take the time to think about it.

But our days of being fooled into spending more are finally over! We have put together common tricks restaurants use to make customers spend more and tips to help you avoid them. If you keep these tips in mind, you will eat great meals in restaurants and never spend a dime more than you have to.

Use overly descriptive language

The use of flowery language on the menu makes dishes appear more tantalizing. Who wouldn't be enticed by words like hand-selected, golden brown, triple-blasted, handcrafted, and slow-cooked, among others? Not you anymore!

According to research conducted by Cornell University, menu items described in a flowery language tend to be more popular and alluring to the customers.[17]

A further study conducted by the University of Illinois revealed that extremely descriptive menu labels increased sales by 27 percent.[18]

Using brand names when describing menu items also increases sales, and that is why chain restaurants like TGI Fridays have Minute Maid orange juice and Jack Daniel's sauce on their menus.

Also, customers get drawn to items described with names of relatives, as they arouse trust and nostalgia. So, menu items like Aunt Jenna's famous potato salad or Grandma's homemade cookies are common in menus.

> Always concentrate on the actual qualities described in the dish and disregard the flowery language. Tangibles can include ingredients, cooking method, and flavor.

Leave out the dollar sign ($)

A dollar sign on the menu is bad for business because it reminds you that you are spending money. Once you realize that you are spending cash, you will pay more attention and base your decisions on the cost of each item.

But the restaurants want you to focus on the dining experience rather than the cost and that is why they will conveniently leave out the dollar sign on the prices.

The Cornell study found that customers given menus with a dollar sign spent considerably less than guests who were given menus without dollar signs.

> Always set your spending ceiling before you withdraw money to go out for a meal.

Highlight items with higher profits

Menu engineers are quite a shrewd lot.

These people know that if they write some dishes in bold, use a fancy colored font, or put them in a box, your eyes will be lured to these items first, as they seem more special than others.

What you don't know is this is a conspiracy to make you spend more because what you think is special is really just expensive.

> Always go through the listed items before you even glance at the "specials."

Offer dishes in two portion sizes

Bracketing is a strategy used by most restaurants whereby they offer foods in two sizes, half and full. The "half" portion is priced higher compared to its size, which makes the "full" portion appear like a great bargain.

I'll give you an example from a restaurant I just went to. They were selling a small portion of French fries for $6, and a large portion for $10 (this was at a ski resort where food is outrageously expensive). People think, "Well, if I get two small portions for $6, that's $12 total, so the $10 large portion must be the better deal."

The customer, with no knowledge of how big the "full" version is, will order the full size assuming that it offers them the best value for the money. What the customer doesn't understand is the restaurant wants to sell the "full" portion, and that is why they put the unreasonably priced "half" portion on the menu so that you can use it as a comparison.

> How full is that "full" portion? Ask the waiter to show you the dish so you can decide if it is actually a good deal.

Offer extremely expensive items

Menu engineers can play with our psychology.

Restaurants include unreasonably priced items on the menu to act as decoys. The main reason for these expensive dishes is to make everything else on the menu look cheaper and therefore something of a bargain.

> Keep away from all the expensive items displayed near the very expensive meals.

Hide value items

Restaurants have analyzed the reading patterns of customers. They place their most profitable dishes in the upper right-hand area of the menu because that is where the eyes of guests will go first.

Most customers, having started reading from the upper right-hand corner, tend to overlook the bottom left area, so that is where menu designers place items that give the restaurant little profit.

> When carefully reading the menu, always start with the bottom left corner.

Use ambiance to increase sales

Restaurants tempt you to spend more by playing you soothing classical music as you dine.

Research by the University of Leicester has revealed that guests are persuaded to spend more when you play classical music, as it makes them feel wealthier.[19]

> **Tip:** If you find a restaurant playing classical music, try to make a decision on what to order using the display menu outside.

Strategically set the buffet

Why do most buffets start with bread and salad?

A salad buffet is meant to make you fill your plate with low-cost food items so that by the time you reach the costly meat counter, your plate has no space to stuff these! You will end up consuming a much cheaper meal than what you paid for.

> **Tip:** To ensure you get the best value for your money, always start with the costlier items like meat first.

Eating out once in a while is a good thing. Keep these tips in your mind before entering any restaurant, and you will keep more of your hard-earned money.

Saving Steps

- Pick a dollar amount you'll spend this month eating out and get this amount of cash out of the ATM for your eating-out money
- Figure out which meals you'll be eating out over the next week to break the habit of mindlessly spending money on food that doesn't bring you pleasure
- Determine what parts of a meal you like the best and spend more on that and less on other items (like soup)

Hardly anyone I ask knows how much they spend on eating out each month. I admit, at one time I didn't either. To build your savings quickly, you'll need all of these tips in your toolbox. And when you have a family, the savings can become even bigger. Turn the page and find out how!

10

Family and Children

The average cost of raising a child now is $233,610, not including college.[20] Yikes! We had twins and my wife managed to save us thousands of dollars over their first few years (they just turned five as this book is being written). Here's how she did it.

Shopping for Baby

We had boy/girl twins in the fall of 2013. While having two children is never going to be inexpensive, here are ideas to save money on prepping for and raising happy babies.

What to buy used

We bought many used items that were still in great shape and saved at a minimum 50 percent and sometimes over 75 percent over new items.

Cribs – Buy your crib on Craigslist. It may have a few scrapes and bite marks, but you can save 75 percent and use that money elsewhere. If you are worried about safety, look up models online and shop for items recently manufactured.

Changing Tables – This is another frequently used parenting item that doesn't get much wear and tear. We got a great one for $20, while even the cheapest models on Amazon cost close to $90.

Car Seats – All car seats must now have expiration dates, so be sure to check them. We found two for 50 percent off the new price, and they looked amazing, as the couple had used them for less than a year. My wife then sold the seats to someone else nine months later because our babies grew so fast. If you don't want to buy a seat used, consider buying a convertible one that can grow with your children or selling your new seat after you are finished using it. If you do buy used, buy from a trusted source because you don't want to buy seats that have been in a crash.

Stroller – We bought the super fancy City Select Stroller with an extra seat on Craigslist for $400, while a new one would have been $800. When we no longer needed it, we sold it for the same $400. We basically rented a fancy stroller for three years for free.

Toys – Hit up a local resale shop for baby toys. It was shocking to us that an activity mat could cost $60 new at Target. You know your babies are going to spit up on these items as soon as you get it out of the box. You might need to wash toys bought at a resale shop before using, but you will save a ton on items that will soon need to be rewashed anyway. It's also hard to resell toys you have purchased new, so start with used.

Clothes – It is great to have new baby clothes, but they are quickly soiled. Buy a majority of your baby's clothes from inexpensive stores or from kid resale shops. Instead of paying $18 for that new outfit junior is going to have a blowout in, buy one from a consignment shop for $7.

Everything You Can Imagine – Join your local Facebook sales groups for baby and children's items. You can even request things you need. You do have to be fast and be able to pick things up.

When and where you shop

For new items here are some ways to save:

New clothes – Watch for sales at the kid clothing stores and the many coupons they will mail out or post online. A 25 percent savings can add up when buying Easter clothes for your kids.

Wipes – Amazon, Costco, and Walmart have good prices on wipes. We love the Costco wipes—they sell 900 wipes for $20. That's about two cents a wipe, and they are great!

Formula (Basic) – If you can and want to breastfeed, do it! Our twins were two months premature, and we used preemie formula until their due dates and then asked our doctor if we could switch to Costco brand. He approved and our kids did great on it.

Formula (Fancy Blends) – While discussing formula with our doctor, he mentioned that fancy formula blends could be simple items just blended for you. For example, some acid reflux formulas are formula with rice cereal blended in. If your child is only doing well on a very expensive formula, ask your doctor what makes that formula special. If it is just a blend of cheaper items, ask your doctor about alternatives.

Things to make

My wife doesn't have a lot of craft talent, but she did bust out her great-grandmother's sewing machine and make curtains and crib skirts from fabric she ordered online. She also got cheap burp cloths and sewed a band of the nursery fabric on each to make them custom. They don't have to be perfect to be pretty.

Curtains – Curtains are a basic pattern and not too hard if you want to sew yourself.

Crib skirts and bumpers – My wife sewed the crib skirts, but bumpers were too hard. Ask a friend or family member with a talent for sewing if they would help you decorate.

Custom burp clothes – You can sew a pretty design or strip of fabric on basic, white burp cloths.

Art – My wife ordered fabric for the room and then friends used some of the extra to make art squares for the wall by covering inexpensive painting canvases. A couple had the kids names on them. They look great and, of course, match perfectly because all the material came in the same order.

Changing table baskets – Buy inexpensive baskets and then pretty them up by adding a little custom detail.

Embroidery – Ask around and see if a friend or family member has a sewing machine that can do embroidery. Sewing machines are now computers, and some can be easily programmed to do what you want.

Decorative pillows / Changing pad cover – Using the same order of fabric as mentioned earlier, my wife's sister-in-law made amazing pillows for the two cribs. This was much less expensive than buying premade pillows. Pillows don't have to be super fancy. You can sew a square or rectangle and fill it with fluff. Changing pad covers can be made by sewing elastic onto your fabric. Make a few and you've saved a bundle of cash, and your nursery will be unique.

DIY paint – A new paint color can make all the difference, and if you or your spouse can paint the nursery, it will save money and make the room unique. I found that there were many helpful blogs on how to add designs to the walls and what colors would look good.

Things to borrow

If you have a group of friends who are also in the baby phase of life, try to borrow a few big-ticket items. There are a few things that we used, and we had no worries about returning.

Swings – If you have twins, you may need two swings to help settle little ones to sleep. These are very expensive, and you only use them for a few months. Our friends let us borrow two swings. Our son wanted to live in one, but our daughter didn't like to swing at all, so I'm glad we didn't buy two.

Exersaucers / play mats – As I mentioned earlier, play mats and other toys can be very expensive and are only used for a short time. Expensive toys that you might borrow are Exersaucers, jumping seats, and play mats. These toys will all get spit up upon and many parents are glad to loan them temporarily to get them out of their house in between babies. You can try to resell new toys you buy, but you will not get much for them. If you can't borrow these items, remember to look for them at kid resale shops.

Parenting books – Most people only read parenting books once. Ask around to see if people have copies of books they recommend that they could loan you. Or just visit your local library.

Things to possibly borrow

Not everyone is comfortable borrowing more personal items, but if it doesn't bother you to ask, you could save a good deal of money.

Baby clothes – We did borrow baby clothes from kind friends, and this can expand your children's wardrobe. My wife found it very stressful as you never know what kind of explosion might happen all over borrowed clothing. If your friends don't mind not getting a few things back and you are comfortable doing it, borrow away. Mark the clothes and keep good track of them so you can return to the right people.

Breast pump – The pump part of a breast pump can be easily borrowed or bought used since it doesn't touch Mom. Many insurance companies now cover breast pumps so ask before purchasing.

Maternity clothes – If you work in an office and need to dress business professional or casual, maternity clothes can add up. Ask around and see if other moms have held onto their clothes and wouldn't mind loaning them. If not, check consignment stores in the area. Also, realize that no one will care if you wear the same few outfits repeatedly towards the end.

Things *not* to buy

Small bottles – We had twins and bottle fed them every three hours. That was a lot of bottles. We took the advice of another twin mom and didn't buy the four-ounce bottles. It did look silly to use an eight-ounce bottle to feed three ounces, but our preemies grew quickly and were soon drinking more. Just buy the larger size and skip the small.

Wipe warmer – Your babies will never know what they are missing if they never have pre-warmed wipes. They *will* notice the difference if you always use a warmer and then go out. You can always take a second to warm up the wipe with the heat of your hand.

Also, some wipe warmers have been known to be fire hazards. There have been too many fires and reports of problems, says consumer advocate Alan Fields, who advises against these products.[21] It's an unnecessary risk for something most kids can do without.

Baby bathtub – Every home comes with a preinstalled baby bathtub called a sink. Also, many hospitals give new parents baby bathtubs before they leave the hospital. Feel free to register for something awesome, but if you don't get it, consider skipping the tub.

Toy storage – Before you run out and buy clever toy storage solutions, consider what you might already have. Many ottomans already have storage spaces. We had a decorative trunk in the living room we just converted to a toy chest. Also, after the babies get a bit older, you will have a better understanding of where it is comfortable for you to let them play. Put storage on a back burner until your house has settled into a routine.

Shoes – Baby shoes might be cute, but babies have no reason to wear them, and there are too many socks out there to spend money on baby shoes. You may also save your sanity because you won't be having to constantly put the shoes back on.

Fancy formula – I've mentioned formula many times, but it is very expensive even if you need it for only one child. Don't be suckered into buying super premium formulas. They are all regulated by the government and unless your doctor specifically recommends a fancy formula for your child, just don't do it.

Tips and tricks

Here are a few miscellaneous tips and tricks we used to spend less.

Travel car seats – Once your kids get older, you can buy travel car seats that fold up and can fit in your carry-on bag for air travel. We bring ours everywhere we fly. You can save on the outrageous costs of renting car seats from a rental car agency, where they stick it to you for $20 a day.

Buy portable high chairs – We bought two $35 portable high chairs from Target and just strapped them onto existing chairs. This saved space with our twins. When we visited someone's house, we could take our chairs with us and corral the monsters at dinner time. As a bonus, these can become booster seats as the kids get older.

Glass bottles – My wife was really drawn to glass bottles as she felt plastic ones got cloudy and filmy after a lot of use. Glass bottles were hard to find, but she got them online at Target. They were much less expensive than fancy plastic bottles. Glass bottles can also be washed on both levels of the dishwasher, a great help when you have thirty-six bottles to wash. Glass bottles don't usually have a million tiny parts that require washing with miniscule instruments.

Photo package – My wife hired a photographer who offered a baby special and took my children's pictures six times in the first year. The package deal was much less expensive than hiring a photographer for each milestone. She also gave discounts for us on other photo sessions if we wanted them.

Get digital picture rights – If you have professional photos done, hire a photographer that will give you the digital rights to print your pictures. My wife was suckered into a Santa session that was very inexpensive but then later found the photographer wanted her to buy all the photos from her at ridiculous prices. I understand that is how some photographers work, but I'd rather find someone who will just take the flat fee and let us print what we want.

Hang dry kids clothes – We found that drying our babies' clothes in the dryer was a sure way to shrink them so they didn't fit anymore. This was especially frustrating when my wife had splurged on the item at a baby store. Your kids are growing and if you have bought new items for them or anything pricey, take the time to hang it dry so that it will continue to look good and will wear longer. You can simply take the clothes out of the washer and put them directly on hangers and allow them to air dry.

Daycare versus nanny – Putting twins into daycare five days a week cost the same as a live-in nanny in our area. The cost blew my mind. Also, with daycare, you must pack everything up to take it with you, bring it all home, wash everything, and repack for the next day. Live-in nannies can be less expensive than day nannies as they get a free place to stay with you.

If you have multiples or have two children in daycare, it is something to consider. Nannies keep small babies at home and perhaps keep them from getting sick. This was important to us when our preemies came home in the middle of winter. Also, nannies can do laundry, wash bottles, and help out in other ways. We used Care.com for hiring childcare professionals and would recommend them as a place to look at your options.

Register for everything and keep receipts – Many stores will offer a discount on registry items that you do not receive as gifts. Also, items on the registry are easier to return or swap. Keep all your receipts. Remember, one baby may love something, like glass bottles, and the other baby may not. You may also find that you don't use as many items as you thought. My wife was told to buy 1001 swaddle cloths, which were very expensive, but my kids kept them clean and we didn't use that many in a week. Saving receipts allows you to be flexible based on your children's likes and dislikes.

Saving Money on Sanity

You've got kids and want to get out of the house! Here are some ideas to save on saving your sanity.

Use family – I know it is obvious, and sometimes easier said than done, but put minor conflict aside and let the family watch the kids.

Swap sitting time – Ask friends with kids if they would be willing to alternate babysitting duties. Watching someone else's children one Friday so we can have the next Friday off is worth it.

Neighbors – Some neighbors definitely don't want to babysit. Since our kids go to bed at 7:30, asking a neighbor to come over and watch TV at our house while our kids sleep is a different story. My wife did this for a friend and she had a super relaxing evening for herself. She got to read a book in a quiet house and didn't have to do any chores. Win-win!

Get thee to the church/house of worship – When they were tiny, getting twins to church was very overwhelming. We stayed home a lot, especially since we didn't want them sick when they first arrived home. When they got to be a year and a half, we enjoyed the time in adult church while they got to play and have fun with friends. We get to see our friends and their children afterward. Bonus: the kids come home tired.

Go to the gym – Yes, the gym daycare may look less than stellar. The tradeoff of an hour working out by yourself, whether in class or just strolling on the treadmill watching TV, is likely worth it. We used to go to an inexpensive gym, and the childcare room didn't look great, but the kids never came home sick and after a few trips, they ran into the room ready to play.

Mother's Day Out programs – If you can't afford daycare and need some time to get things done without the kids, Mother's Day Out programs can be an affordable choice. They are usually two half-days a week. If your kids are always home with you, they may enjoy some new toys and friends to play with, as well.

Remember what life is about – Finally, remember that time with your babies does not require fancy clothes, new toys, organic food, or whatever society is pressuring you to spend money on.

Remind yourself that just over a hundred years ago, your great-grandparents were raising children on farms and pasture lands without iPads, TV shows, "learning toys," professional photographers, and birthday parties for 100. Your kids need *you* and your love, and that is all that matters.

Make Your Own Baby Food

When we first started on baby food, we bought it at the store because my wife was tired and overwhelmed. But our two little babies were turning into voracious eaters and buying at the store was getting expensive very quickly. When she had to buy $50 in baby food to feed the kids for less than a week, she started roasting, steaming, and blending foods she was cooking anyway. Making baby food does not have to be special or fancy. Just roast food in the oven or stream it on the stove and then use a food processor to blend it. There is no need to buy special kitchen equipment. We saved thousands of dollars by spending time in the kitchen. It's worth it and also super healthy for your kids.

> A side bonus is you won't have picky eaters. Katie often blended with water the same food we were eating. Our twins were exposed to pizza, Thai food, hamburgers, and all kinds of vegetables before they ever held a spoon.

If you make baby food, please don't get sucked into buying special baby food holders at the baby store. Go to Amazon.com or Walmart and buy 4oz or 8oz jelly jars and fill them. They can be frozen and put in the microwave, and they cost a fraction of specialty baby food systems.

Diapers

Diapers will be one of your biggest expenses. These are some tips on how you can trim the costs.

Consider buying diapers from Costco or Sam's Club. We bought pricey Pampers while our kids were tiny but soon found Costco diapers did just fine for us. Also check out Amazon Mom at Amazon.com. Amazon Mom members get 20 percent off diaper subscriptions and other deals. Try a small sample of generic diapers and see if they work well on your child. Every kid is different, and you might luck out with a child who can do well in the generic diapers.

Get free diapers

Baby diapers are very expensive, and anyone with children knows that if you don't look for deals, you can end up spending hundreds of dollars per month for diapers. Here are some options for free diapers.

Double coupons and sales

Savvy diaper shoppers already know that using coupons is a must when shopping for deals. But you may not know that using coupons can actually net you free baby diapers!

The first thing you need to do is look for sales. Many stores price match products from other stores, so be sure to use that to your advantage. Once you find a good sale, it's time to find some coupons.

Search online, check your local newspaper, or sign up with diaper companies to receive manufacturer coupons. Once you have the coupons, it's time to find a double coupon event. Often you can find these at retail outlets.

Combine the sale (price match if you must) with double coupons, and you'll be on your way to another batch of free diapers! If you can get multiple coupons, have some of your friends go with you to purchase even more.

Non-profit and low-income organizations

There are many non-profit organizations that help people get free baby diapers. Typically, those organizations include:

- churches
- local or state low-income organizations
- diaper banks

If you have little or no income, there are many local and state programs that are designed to help low-income families get the help they need.

Free samples

Getting free samples is one of the easiest ways to get free baby diapers. Diaper manufacturers obviously want consumers to use their brand, so they will send out free samples for people to try.

They usually limit samples on a per-household basis, but if you have some friends that will sign up and give you their free samples, you may end up with many free baby diapers.

You can order free samples from the diaper manufacturers' websites.

Diaper banks

Diaper banks take donations from other people, as well as companies and diaper manufacturers, and then distribute the diapers to people who request them. The available inventory depends on donations, so the amount and type of diapers you receive varies.

You can find more information and locations at the National Diaper Bank Network.

Medical institutions

Medical institutions such as the doctor's offices and hospitals frequently get free samples of diapers from manufacturers to distribute to patients. Since those samples are usually samples of new products, there is no guarantee about what types or sizes are available, but if you call local doctors and hospitals in your area, you can find out what's currently available.

Switch to cloth diapers

Cloth diapers are not as popular as they once were due to the messiness of cleaning them, but if you really want free baby diapers, this is a great solution because you can reuse them over and over again.

You really start saving if you plan on having multiple kids because the diapers can be reused from child to child.

Potty train – now

I met three-year-old twin boys at the playground once. I noticed both had diapers on. Ka-ching!

My son was potty trained at 1 1/2, my daughter at age 2. They still had diapers for naps and nighttime, but that's a combined **2 1/2 years** we didn't buy diapers (compared to the family at the playground), which adds up to over $2,000 in savings.

It takes longer to potty train younger kids, but the savings make it worth it.

Pets

Cancel pet insurance

You will hear stories of people who have bought pet insurance and how great it was when their pet got sick. These stories are the exception, not the rule.

When you review pet insurance, you will find many caps and limits on what they cover. Along with the high deductibles, it becomes a bad deal. You're much better off saving the amount you would be paying for insurance into a pet fund to cover any issues for Fido and Fluffy.

Saving Steps

- Start using Craigslist and Facebook groups as the first store you visit
- Make your own baby food using the food you eat and a blender
- Commit to potty training starting no later than 2-years old

Let's bust open one of the ways you can get more in your paycheck next week and uncover some forgotten funds. Let's get to finding money you may not even know about.

11

Find Extra Money

When you are thinking about savings, do you ever wonder if there is something you could do to get extra cash right now? In the world of saving, there are the things that require lots of work (like extreme couponing) and the little, hidden things most people have never heard about. Read on. There might be some hidden money under a rock you missed.

Turn Gift Cards into Cash

Gift cards are real money you might have lying around in your junk drawer. Sell them and get some cash to spend on what you really want. The sites listed below take a small cut, but it's better than having a piece of plastic you might never use.

And if you routinely shop somewhere, buy a discounted gift card and save money. There are websites where you can buy gift cards for less than their face value.

For example, Raise.com sells discount gift cards or electronic gift cards. Here are just a few examples from Raise.com:

- Walmart – Save 4 percent
- Target – Save 6 percent
- Home Depot – Save 6 percent
- Starbucks – Save 15 percent

Cardpool.com is another website where you can buy discounted gift cards up to 35 percent off, sell gift cards for cash, or trade gift cards. It is the most trusted and most popular gift card exchange.

Bring Home More Money in Your Paycheck

If you're getting a tax refund, you're giving the government an interest-free loan.

According to the IRS website, **the average tax refund is $3,034.**

That means people are letting the federal government borrow, tax-free, $252.00 *each month*. That's money they could use towards getting out of debt, saving for the future, or building wealth. On average you can get an extra $250/month in your paycheck by adjusting your withholding.

You should earn the interest on *your* money, not loan it out for free.

How would you like to see your paycheck increase next week?

This is one of those things you don't want to procrastinate about. Your next paycheck is coming up fast. It might take you twenty minutes.

You can get an estimate of how much you can save by using the withholding calculator at irs.gov. Once you've used the withholding calculator, you will need to fill out a new W-4 with your employer to have the correct amount withheld from your paycheck.

You filled out a W-4 when you first started working wherever you are currently employed. It's time to fill out a new one and start keeping your money.

That's all there is to it. You tell your employer you want them to take fewer taxes out of your paycheck each week. If you do this, you will no longer be overpaying each week on your taxes.

You will have more take-home cash by your next paycheck if you adjust your withholding properly today.

Disclaimer – I'm not a licensed CPA, so get your advice about proper withholding from a tax pro if you have any questions before changing your tax withholding. Do it wrong and you may get a massive tax bill next year.

If you're not sure whether you should change your withholding, talk to a local tax preparer. There are certain life events that should trigger a talk with a tax expert.

- If you're getting big refunds, talk with a tax expert.
- If you are moving from an apartment into a new house with a mortgage payment, talk with a tax expert.

- If you just had another child, talk with a tax expert.
- If you just got married or divorced, talk with a tax expert.

Any type of life-changing event should result in you talking with a tax expert so you can keep more of your paycheck.

Find Missing Money

A relative of mine was tracked down by E-Trade, an online investment brokerage. It turns out he had an investment account with **$900** in it that he had completely forgotten about.

Is there money just waiting out there for you? Finding free money is just one way to get extra money fast.

$60 billion - Estimated amount of unclaimed money according to the National Unclaimed Property Authority.[22]

$1billion- According to the Florida Sentinel, Florida residents alone have **$1 billion** of unclaimed and forgotten money.[23]

This is money from:

- old employers
- local governments
- investment firms
- insurance companies
- utility companies
- banks
- mortgage companies

and it goes back as much as twenty years!

It's legitimate money. The owners couldn't be located so the money goes unclaimed. The money is held in the unclaimed property division of each state.

> All totaled in the US there are *billions* and *billions* of dollars in unclaimed money waiting to be collected by people like you.

How you can find missing money

Visit missingmoney.com and you can search for your name or a relatives name. Search for every state you've lived in to see if anything comes up.

If you have a common name like John Smith, it may take you more digging to see if there is anything for you. If you have a unique name like Schwarzenegger, your search will go a little quicker.

Is this for every state?

There are a few states that don't participate in missingmoney.com. The easiest way to find out if a state participates is to visit the website and click on the searchable map.

For those states that don't participate, you can Google the state name and "unclaimed property" (for example, "Georgia unclaimed property").

Read the search instructions if you have to visit a state-specific website. On the Georgia website, you have to enter your last name first, but the web page just asks for a name. If you don't do the search correctly, you could miss out.

How much does it cost?

That's the best part about it—using missingmoney.com is completely free!

> I found $100 that had gone missing! It took me about two minutes to fill out the claim form and print it. The money was a credit card refund/rebate that had been sent to the wrong address. I also searched for one of my relatives. I found a $20 refund from the power company that had been unclaimed.

Hidden Discounts

You may not be aware of all the discounts that might be available to you from:

- your employer
- being a member of a warehouse club
- organizations you are a part of (such as AAA or AARP)

Some of the discounts you could be missing out on include:

- Free warehouse club memberships
- Cheaper cell phone plans
- Discounted auto insurance
- Discounted travel and car rental rates
- Incentives for healthy lifestyle choices

- Gym memberships
- Free flu shots
- Tuition reimbursement

Speak with the human resources rep at your company and ask for a list of all the perks you could be missing.

> My old company used to give us free Sam's Club memberships as a perk.

Saving Steps

- Go through your junk drawers to find and sell old gift cards
- Change your tax withholding if you are getting tax refunds to keep more money in your paycheck
- Visit missingmoney.com and search for yourself, your friends, and family for any forgotten money
- Contact the human resources department at your employer and organizations you're a member of to get a list of discounts and perks available

While all of the previous tips will save you money, there are some purchases that can cost you more in the long run. So let's turn the page and finish our savings journey with the things you should never sacrifice quality on.

12

The Splurge List

I saw a TV segment once of a guy who lived on next to nothing. Ultra cheap. The camera man showed him hanging up used paper towels on a clothesline to dry out and be reused.

That was not my vision of financial freedom. Not my vision of anything, except a guy with a miserable life spending his time washing paper towels.

Sometimes spending some extra money can save you time or money, or gain you comfort, in the long run. There are a lot of little things that make a big difference in the quality of your life.

Buy the best quality you can afford.

For example, if you buy a great chef's knife, you'll never have to buy another one again in your life. I've had my $200 Kitchen Aid mixer (because I like to bake) for fifteen years.

What are some things you should consider paying extra for?

Things to Splurge On

1. Cookware

When we got married, a lot of high-quality cookware was on our gift registry. We didn't get much of it as gifts, so we bought what we needed ourselves. (Bonus: when you create a gift registry at stores like Macy's, you often get a 10 percent or greater discount on the items you didn't get.)

If you like cooking and do it often, paying for cookware that will last a long time can help you be a more efficient cook. Check for products that include a lifetime warranty. One of the knives we bought started to rust, so we shipped it back to the manufacturer for a free replacement.

Yes, quality costs more but if you get a warranty, you'll never have to buy a replacement.

If you can't yet afford a lot of higher-priced kitchen items, buy them one at a time.

2. Coffee Maker

Do you think paying $200 for a Nespresso machine is too much? If a pod costs $1 and you compare that to a $5 coffee on your way to work, the payback is pretty quick. The expensive coffee maker will pay off in the long run.

Higher-priced coffeemakers generally have better water filtration systems and higher boiling points, which make the coffee better for you and better tasting.[24]

3. Toilet Paper

When you go to a restaurant, rest stop, or the airport and are forced to use the cheap, harsh toilet paper, you notice, don't you?

I believe you deserve the best.

You can find great deals by buying in bulk at the warehouse clubs. Make sure to shop around. *Amazon often does not have the best prices on toilet paper.*

4. Shoes

A high-quality pair of shoes can last a lot longer than cheap ones, which you have to replace every six months. This is especially true of sneakers if you exercise or walk around a lot.

That doesn't mean springing $250 for the latest Air Jordans for your kids. But a good brand of sneakers for your kids will likely do better than the $15 special at Walmart.

I owned a pair of Doc Martins ($110) that I wore for two years in college and another eight years after graduating. They were dressy enough to wear to work every day at my corporate job.

5. Food

You may occasionally save money by eating cheap, processed foods. But you will pay later when health issues catch up to you due to excessive weight, clogged arteries, or diabetes. Higher-priced, good-quality food is cheaper in the long run than doctor's visits and hospital time. Not to mention you'll have more energy and you'll feel better.

Here are a few ideas:

- Butter over margarine
- Olive oil over vegetable oil (or Crisco)
- Whole wheat over enriched white flour
- Fresh produce over canned
- Pure honey and maple syrup over high-fructose corn syrup
- All-natural peanut butter over Jif/Skippy

Be wary of labels such as *all natural and whole grains*. Those are marketing terms to make you think something is healthy. The easy way to know if something is good for you or not is to read the ingredient list. If you can pronounce all the ingredients and it doesn't read like a chemistry textbook, you're in good shape.

6. Office Chair

Do you have back problems? Maybe you've heard sitting is the new cancer. Sitting at a desk for long periods can be tough on your lower back.

A good chair goes a long way to keeping you comfortable and pain-free at work.

My wedding present from Katie was a $750 Aeron office chair. I sat in that chair eight to fifteen hours a day for nine years until I switched to my stand-up desk. That comes out to a fraction of a penny per hour to help prevent back pain.

What's Not Worth Splurging On

Some products are so heavily marketed and advertised, they make you feel bad when you don't spend large sums of money on them. Here are two items I've found (and verified with Consumer Reports) that most people overspend on.

1. Pet food

Just like you, your pets deserve the best. I love my pets and buy them high-quality food. But research shows the difference between premium and cheap pet food is "In many cases, the companies' profits are higher, but your pet's health is no different."[25]

I'm not buying Great Value brand from Walmart, but I'm not feeding my dog refrigerated grilled Kobe beef either.

Buy the best value for your spending plan when it comes to pet food. The pet food industry wants to make us think we are terrible pet parents if we don't spend obscene amounts of money on their clever marketing for fancy ingredients.

2. Mattresses

You can find great mattresses for cheap at Walmart and Costco. So you're not splurging. There are comfortable, great-quality mattresses for $300 to $400, depending on what size you need. You're only splurging if you fall for the marketing hype that a $800+ mattress will give you a better night's sleep.

Costco has great $400 memory foam mattresses from Novaform that are just as comfortable as a $2,000 Tempur-Pedic.

3. Sheets

If you wear pajamas to bed, what percent of your body actually touches the sheets? The answer is not much. If you want to splurge on something, buy an expensive pillow case so your face is comfortable.

We get our sheets at Bed, Bath & Beyond using one of the 20-percent-off coupons.

The nice thing is BB&B will replace the sheets if something goes wrong. I was rolling over one night, and my elbow ripped a hole right through the fitted sheet. Katie brought it back and got a free replacement.

Sometimes, quality and comfort matter. If you've got the buffer in your spending plan, you can save money in the long run by spending extra now. Check out online reviews of products before you buy, and don't be afraid to return something if you don't like it. If you use common sense and spend a **reasonable** amount of money on stuff, you'll come out ahead.

Spending Steps

- Figure out the things you want to spend more on, and with all of the savings tips you'll have the extra money to do so
- Become a better buyer by paying attention to advertising and marketing, and doing some research and comparison shopping

- Buy the best value you can afford based on your spending plan

This book has over a thousand tips on saving money. Remember that **knowledge is not power, acting on that knowledge is**. Take a few minutes each day to try something new and build your savings habits. This is how I started building wealth, and how you will to.

About The Author

Scott Alan Turner is a former money moron, living the paycheck-to-paycheck lifestyle, losing $40k in the stock market, and racking up a load of credit card debt. But by age 35, he turned it all around and became a self-made millionaire.

In a world of get-rich-quick schemes, biased advice, and financial Pied Pipers, Scott's authentic, no-holds-bared approach makes it possible for anyone to absolutely rock their personal finances.

Scott is on a mad mission to help you get financial independence, ultimate happiness and a life full of awesome experiences. With his rebel style, off-beat humor, and signature life-on-your-own-terms approach, Scott's inspiring a movement of Financial Rock Stars across the globe.

Scott is the bestselling author of *99 Minute Millionaire*, and a CERTIFIED FINANCIAL PLANNER™.

Meet Scott and receive free training and resources at ScottAlanTurner.com

References

1 "CNBC" "A $523 monthly payment is the new standard for car buyers." Accessed February 1, 2019. https://www.cnbc.com/2018/05/31/a-523-monthly-payment-is-the-new-standard-for-car-buyers.html

2 "Insurance.com" "Comprehensive and collision coverage." Accessed February 1, 2019. https://www.insurance.com/auto-insurance/coverage/comprehensive-and-collision-auto-insurance.html

3 "Consumer Reports" "Should You Get an Extended Warranty for Your Car?" Accessed February 1, 2019. https://www.consumerreports.org/used-car-buying/when-an-extended-car-warranty-is-worth-it/

4 "Consumer Reports" "Extended Car Warranties: An Expensive Gamble." Accessed February 1, 2019. https://

www.consumerreports.org/extended-warranties/extended-car-warranties-an-expensive-gamble/

5 "CBS News" "ATM and overdraft fees hit an all-time high." Accessed February 1, 2019. https://www.cnbc.com/2017/10/03/atm-fees-have-hit-a-hig h-heres-how-much-cardholders-are-paying.html

6 "CBS News" "Identity theft has never been more rampant." Accessed February 1, 2019. https://www.cbsnews.com/news/identity-theft-hits-record-high/

7 "Clark.com" "LifeLock is legit, but is it worth your money?" Accessed February 1, 2019. https://clark.com/protect-your-identity/lifelock-credit-freeze/

8 "Consumer Federation of America" "Consumers Need Relief from Debt Settlement Rip-Offs." Accessed February 1, 2019. https://consumerfed.org/press_release/consumers-need-relief-from-debt-settlemen t-rip-offs-consumer-and-privacy-groups-su pport-senate-and-house-bills-to-curb-debt -settlement-abuses/

9 "MNN" "Americans Spend $2k on home energy costs." Accessed February 1, 2019. https://www.mnn.com/money/personal-finance/blogs/americans-spend-2k-on-home-energy-costs-annually

10 "Insurance.com" "Average homeowners insurance rates by state." Accessed February 1, 2019. https://www.insurance.com/home-and-renters-insurance/home-insurance-basics/average-homeowners-insurance-rates-by-state

11 "GO Banking Rates" "Here's Why It Costs $1,204 a Month to Maintain the Average Home." Accessed February 1, 2019. https://

www.gobankingrates.com/investing/real-estate/heres-costs-1126-month-maintain-average-american-home/

12 "Huffington Post" "The Life Insurance Industry's Big Secret." Accessed February 1, 2019. https://www.huffpost.com/entry/the-life-insurance-indust_b_1937246

13 "Water Tech" "How much does bottled water really cost you?" Accessed February 1, 2019. http://blog.watertech.com/how-much-does-bottled-water-cost-you/

14 "How Stuff Works" "How much money can I save with a water filter?" Accessed February 1, 2019. https://home.howstuffworks.com/save-money-with-water-filter1.htm

15 "Consumer Reports" "Store brand foods review." Accessed February 1, 2019. https://www.consumerreports.org/cro/magazine/2013/10/best-store-brands/index.htm

16 "NRDC." "How America Is Losing Up to 40 Percent of Its Food from Farm to Fork to Landfill." Accessed February 1, 2019. https://www.nrdc.org/sites/default/files/wasted-food-IP.pdf

17 "Cornell University." "Descriptive Menu Labels Effect on Sales." Accessed February 1, 2019. https://foodpsychology.cornell.edu/research/descriptive-menu-labels-effect-sales

18 "Cornell University." "Descriptive Menu Labels Effect on Sales." Accessed February 1, 2019. https://foodpsychology.cornell.edu/sites/default/files/unmanaged_files/descriptivemenulabels-2001.pdf

19 "University of Leicester." "Having the right taste for music." Accessed February 1, 2019. https://www.le.ac.uk/press/ebulletin/news/havingtherighttaste.html

20 "Money Magazine." "The Cost of Raising a Child." Accessed February 1, 2019. http://time.com/money/4629700/child-raising-cost-department-of-agriculture-report/

21 "Fields, Alan." "Baby Bargains." Accessed February 1, 2019. http://www.aacpp.com/pdf/Baby-Product-dangers.pdf

22 "NAUPA." "What is Unclaimed Property." Accessed February 1, 2019. https://www.unclaimed.org/what/

23 "Florida Treasure Hunt." "Join Florida's Treasure Hunt." Accessed February 1, 2019. https://www.fltreasurehunt.org/

24 Consumer Reports, "Best Drip Coffee Makers From Consumer Reports' Tests." Accessed February 1, 2019. https://www.consumerreports.org/coffee-makers/best-drip-coffee-makers-consumer-reports-tests/

25 "Tufts University." "Premium pet foods – are they worth the premium price?" Accessed February 1, 2019. http://vetnutrition.tufts.edu/2016/10/should-you-buy-premium-pet-food/

Made in the USA
Monee, IL
08 November 2026

67384903R00114